VEGETARIAN
CUISINE

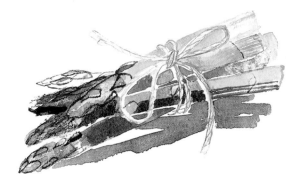

TORMONT

TORMONT

Graphic design: Zapp
Selection of recipes: Marc Maulà

Original recipes and photos:
Ceres Verlag, Rudolf-August Oetker KG, Germany
Quadrillion Publishing Ltd., United Kingdom
Rolli Books, India

Pictured on the front cover: *Salad of Avocado, Grapes, Blue Cheese and Walnuts,* page 16.
Pictured on the back cover: *Mushroom Curry,* page 174.

Canadä

The publisher thanks Heritage Canada for the support awarded
under the Book Publishing Industry Development Program.

Government of Québec–Book Publishing Tax Credit
Program–Administered by SODEC.

Printed in China

Contents

Introduction

An ever-growing number of people are turning to vegetarianism for a variety of reasons – some out of concern for the well-being of animals, others for environmental reasons, and many more for health reasons.

Studies suggest that vegetarians are significantly less likely to develop cancer at an early age than meat eaters. Added to that, because vegetarians and vegans are often slimmer than meat eaters, and because they eat more fiber and more complex carbohydrates in the form of wholegrain cereals, nuts, and pulses that have fewer saturated fats (predominantly found in animal products), they enjoy lower levels of blood cholesterol and therefore heart disease, and they have a higher level of protection against several bowel diseases.

And besides offering a healthy diet, vegetarian food, if well balanced, provides the opportunity to enjoy a whole new taste experience beyond the confines of the traditional meal. This is the chance to explore to the fullest the wealth of fresh and exotic fruits, vegetables, and herbs now freely available all year round, as well as the heady mix of spices and flavorings drawn from the cuisines of the world. Then there are those all-important, nourishing staple foods which offer enormous potential for creating imaginative and delicious dishes – nutty grains such as couscous and wild rice, toothsome tomato and spinach-flavored pasta, sweet nuts such as pistachios and pecans, and tender pulses (legumes) including various beans, lentils, and chickpeas.

This book presents a collection of exciting recipes for all those who enjoy good food, whether they are committed vegetarians or not. Sample the vegetarian highlights of international cooking, such as Spanish Gazpacho soup, Greek Tzatziki dip, Indian Vegetable Curry and Middle Eastern Tabouleh salad, or savor the delights of some contemporary creations including Watercress and Mushroom Paté, Parsnip Fritters, Potato and Zucchini Gratin, and Chocolate and Almond Biscuits. So, why not go vegetarian today?

Mixed Salads

Endive Salad with Black Grapes

This attractive salad is full of varied textures and flavors, enhanced with a lemon yogurt dressing.

Preparation time: 15 minutes · Serves: 4

1 cup	plain yogurt	250 mL
7 tsp	lemon juice	35 mL
4 tsp	chopped lemon balm	20 mL
	salt	
	sugar	
4	small endives, leaves separated	4
4	apples, peeled, cored and sliced	4
4	small orange, peeled and segmented	4
2 tbsp	sunflower seeds	30 mL
½ cup	black grapes	125 mL
	lemon balm leaves, to garnish	

• For the dressing, in a bowl, mix the yogurt with the lemon juice, lemon balm and salt and sugar to taste. Stir the ingredients together to mix well, then set aside.

• Arrange the endive leaves, apple slices and orange segments on a serving plate.

• Sprinkle the salad with sunflower seeds and scatter the grapes on top.

• Garnish with lemon balm leaves and serve with the yogurt dressing spooned into the center of the salad or alongside.

Serving suggestion: Serve with thin slices of wholewheat bread and butter.

Variations: Use 4 pears in place of the apples. Use fresh parsley in place of lemon balm. Use pumpkin seeds in place of the sunflower seeds.

Lollo Rosso Salad

This is a colorful variation on the traditional Greek salad.

Preparation time: 10 minutes · Serves: 4

½	bunch of Lollo Rosso (red-leaf) lettuce	½
3	medium tomatoes, diced	3
1	red pepper, seeded and chopped	1
1	green pepper, seeded and chopped	1
3	sticks of celery, sliced	3
2 cups	cucumber, diced	500 mL
2 cups	Cheddar cheese, diced or crumbled	500 mL
16	black olives	16
DRESSING		
1½ tbsp	tarragon vinegar	20 mL
¼ cup	olive oil	60 mL

• Break the lettuce into pieces with your fingers and place in a bowl.

• Add the tomato, peppers, celery, cucumber and cheese and stir to mix.

• For the dressing, mix together the vinegar and oil in a small bowl and drizzle over the salad. Toss gently to mix.

• Place the salad on a serving dish and top with the olives. Serve.

Serving suggestion: Serve for lunch with a crusty roll or French bread.

Variations: If you do not like olives, use halved, seeded black grapes instead. Use 4 green onions in place of celery. Use Cheshire cheese in place of Cheddar. Use radishes in place of cucumber.

COOK'S TIP

To keep celery crisp, wash well and place the sticks in a jug of cold water in the refrigerator.

Watercress and Orange Salad

This eye-catching salad combination is ideal served with cold meats or fish.

Preparation time: 20 minutes · Serves: 4–6

3	large bunches of watercress	3
4	oranges	4
6 tbsp	vegetable oil	90 mL
	juice and rind of 1 orange	
	pinch of sugar	
1 tsp	lemon juice	5 mL
	salt and freshly ground black pepper	
	carrots, grated, for garnish	

• Remove any thick stalks from the watercress. Break the watercress into small sprigs, discarding any yellow leaves. Set aside.

• Carefully remove the peel and pith from the oranges using a small sharp knife. Catch any juice that spills in a small bowl.

• Remove the fleshy segments from between the thin membranes inside the oranges. Squeeze any juice from the orange membranes into the bowl with the juice from the peel.

• Arrange the grated carrot and watercress with the orange segments on a serving dish.

• Place the remaining ingredients in the bowl with the reserved orange juice and whisk together with a fork, until thickened.

• Pour the salad dressing over the oranges and watercress just before serving, to prevent the watercress from going limp.

Variations: Use grapefruit in place of oranges. Use chicory in place of watercress.

Salade Bresse

This sophisticated salad is equally good as a first course or as an accompaniment to a main course for a formal summer dinner.

Preparation time: 20 minutes · Serves: 4–6

1	head of radicchio leaves, separated	1
1	head of romaine lettuce	1
1	bunch of lamb's lettuce or watercress	1
⅔ cup	cherry tomatoes, halved and cored	150 mL
¼ lb	Bresse blue, or other blue cheese, cut into small pieces	115 g
16	small pickles, thinly sliced	16
½ cup	walnut halves	125 mL
2 tbsp	each vegetable and walnut oil, mixed	30 mL
2 tbsp	white wine vinegar	30 mL
¾ cup	fromage frais (or quark, or low-fat cottage cheese)	175 mL
2 tsp	chopped fresh tarragon leaves	10 mL
	salt and freshly ground black pepper	

• Tear the radicchio and romaine lettuce leaves into bite-sized pieces. Pull apart the lamb's lettuce but leave the leaves whole. If using watercress, remove and discard any thick stems and yellow leaves. Toss all the salad leaves together in a large salad bowl.

• Add the tomatoes, cheese, pickles and walnuts to the salad bowl and lightly toss to mix.

• Place the oils and wine vinegar in a small bowl and whisk with a fork until thickened. Fold in the fromage frais and the tarragon leaves. Whisk thoroughly, then season to taste with salt and pepper.

• Drizzle some of the dressing over the salad before serving. Serve the salad with the remainder of the dressing in a small jug.

Serving suggestion: Serve with crusty French bread.

Variations: Use your own choice of salad leaves. Use cooked turkey breast in place of chicken. Use thick-set plain yogurt in place of fromage frais.

COOK'S TIP

If you want to prepare this salad in advance, do not add the dressing until the last minute, otherwise the leaves will go limp.

Melon and Cucumber Salad with Roquefort Dressing

A refreshingly fruity salad with a piquant cheese dressing.

Preparation time: 20 minutes · Serves: 4

½	cucumber	½
1	cantaloupe	1
1	lime	1
1	onion	1
	a few sprigs of fresh mint	
1	head of crisp lettuce	1
DRESSING		
¼ lb	Roquefort cheese	125 g
½ cup	sour cream	125 mL
1–2 tbsp	lemon juice	15–30 mL
2–3 tbsp	light (table) cream	30–45 mL
	salt and freshly ground black pepper	

• Peel the cucumber and thinly slice. Set aside.

• Cut the melon in half, remove the skin and seeds, then cut the flesh into neat slices. Set aside

• Remove and discard the peel and white pith from the lime. Thinly slice the flesh and set aside.

• Thinly slice the onion, separate the rings and set aside.

• Remove the leaves from the mint sprigs and set aside.

• Separate the lettuce leaves and arrange on individual serving plates.

• Arrange the cucumber and melon slices on the plates with the lime slices on top. Scatter over the onion rings and mint leaves.

• For the dressing, crumble the cheese into a small bowl, then mix with the sour cream, lemon juice and cream until smooth. Season to taste with salt and pepper.

• Serve the salad with the dressing spooned over.

Serving suggestion: Serve with slices of mixed-grain bread.

Variations: Use papaya or mango in place of melon. Use blue or Stilton cheese in place of Roquefort.

Salad of Avocado, Grapes, Blue Cheese and Walnuts

This colorful salad can be served warm or cold for a snack or light meal.

Preparation time: 20 minutes · Cooking time: 1–2 minutes (microwave on HIGH) · Serves: 4

1	head of curly endive (or friseé lettuce)	1
1	head of chicory	1
1	head of radicchio	1
2	small bunches of lamb's lettuce or watercress	2
1	head of iceberg lettuce	1
2	avocados	2
1 cup	black grapes	250 mL
4 tbsp	fresh mixed herbs, chopped	60 mL
1 cup	walnut pieces	250 mL
¼ lb	blue cheese, diced or crumbled	110 g
3 tbsp	walnut oil and grapeseed oil, mixed	50 mL
2 tbsp	lemon vinegar	30 mL
	pinch of sugar	
	salt and freshly ground black pepper	

COOK'S TIP

It is important to tear the endive, chicory and radicchio by hand, since the edges will discolor if they are cut with a knife.

• Tear the endive, chicory and radicchio into small pieces and place in a bowl.

• If using lamb's lettuce, separate the leaves. If using watercress, remove any thick stalks. Add to the bowl with the endive mixture.

• Shred the iceberg lettuce with a sharp knife and add to the bowl.

• Peel and pit the avocado, then cut into neat slices. Carefully toss with the salad leaves.

• Cut the grapes in half; remove and discard any seeds. Add the grapes to the bowl of salad.

• Finally, toss the chopped herbs, walnut pieces and diced cheese into the salad, taking care not to break up the pieces of avocado.

• Place the oils, vinegar, sugar and seasoning in a clean screw-top jar. Screw the lid on tightly and shake the jar vigorously until the dressing is well blended.

• Drizzle the dressing over the salad and toss lightly to mix.

• Arrange the salad in equal amounts on 4 serving plates.

• Heat each plate in a microwave oven on HIGH for 1–2 minutes just before serving, if you like. Serve immediately.

Serving suggestion: Serve with slices of crusty wholewheat bread.

Variations: For a vegan alternative, use 3 cups (750 mL) wild mushrooms (in place of the blue cheese) cooked in 2 tbsp (60 mL) white wine, drained and chilled. Use 2 medium mangos in place of the avocados.

Summer Salad with Blue Cheese Cream

A wonderfully elegant dish for a special summer meal.

Preparation time: 15 minutes · Serves: 4

1	head of leaf lettuce, leaves separated	1
1	bunch of radishes	1
½	medium cucumber	½
10	stuffed green olives	10
½ cup	blue cheese, cubed or crumbled	125 mL
2 tbsp	sour cream	30 mL
3 tbsp	olive oil	45 mL
2 tbsp	white wine vinegar	30 mL
	freshly ground black pepper	
	sugar	
1 tbsp	fresh herbs, finely chopped	15 mL

• Tear the larger lettuce leaves into pieces and place all the lettuce in a salad bowl.

• Trim the radishes. Thinly slice larger radishes and cut smaller radishes into quarters. Add to the salad bowl.

• Cut the cucumber in half lengthwise, remove the seeds and cut the flesh into slices about ½ in (1 cm) thick. Add to the salad bowl.

• Cut half of the olives in half and finely slice the remainder. Add the halved olives to the other salad ingredients.

• For the dressing, press the cheese through a sieve into a small bowl. Whisk with the sour cream, oil and wine vinegar until smooth.

• Add to the dressing the sliced olives, pepper and sugar to taste, and the chopped herbs.

• Spoon the dressing over the salad before serving.

Serving suggestion: An excellent salad to go with cold poached salmon or smoked salmon.

Variations: Use halved cherry tomatoes in place of radishes. Use black olives or garlic and lemon marinated olives in place of stuffed olives.

COOK'S TIP

Use ripe Stilton or Roquefort instead of blue cheese for the dressing.

Feta Salad

This delectable salad is distinctly Greek in origin. Serve it as a substantial starter or as a light lunch.

Preparation time: 15 minutes · Serves: 4

½	small head of curly endive (or chickory)	½
½	small iceberg lettuce	½
1	small cucumber	1
4	large tomatoes	4
8–10	green or black olives, pitted and halved	8–10
1	medium Spanish or red onion, sliced	1
¼ lb	Feta cheese	115 g
5 tbsp	olive oil	75 mL
2 tbsp	red wine vinegar	30 mL
1 tsp	fresh marjoram (or oregano), chopped	5 mL
½ tsp	freshly ground sea salt	2 mL
¼ tsp	freshly ground black pepper	1 mL
½ tsp	prepared mustard	2 mL

- Tear the endive and lettuce into bite-sized pieces and set aside.

- Thinly slice the cucumber and set aside.

- Cut a small cross in the top of each tomato and plunge into boiling water for 30 seconds, then immerse in cold water. Using a small sharp knife, remove the skins from the tomatoes, then slice the flesh crosswise.

- Place the endive, lettuce, cucumber, tomatoes, olives and onion in a serving bowl. Toss together until thoroughly mixed.

- Cut the cheese into ½-in (1-cm) cubes. Scatter over the salad in the serving bowl.

- Place the remaining ingredients in a small bowl and whisk together with a fork, until thickened.

- Pour the dressing over the salad and serve immediately.

Serving suggestions: Serve with baked potatoes or with warmed or toasted pita bread.

Variations: Use Haloumi, Cheddar or Cheshire cheese in place of Feta. Use fresh flat-leafed parsley or chives in place of marjoram or oregano.

Greek Salad

A classic and ever-appealing salad of marinated vegetables and Feta cheese.

Preparation time: 15 minutes, plus marinating time · Cooking time: 5–10 minutes · Serves: 4–6

4 tbsp	olive oil	60 mL
4 small	zucchinis, sliced	4
1 tbsp	fresh dill, finely chopped	15 mL
2 tbsp	walnut oil	30 mL
2 tbsp	fresh lemon juice	30 mL
1 tbsp	tarragon vinegar	15 mL
4	large tomatoes, skinned	4
1	red pepper, seeded	1
1	green pepper, seeded	1
2	onions	2
2½ cups	Feta cheese, crumbled	625 mL
2 tbsp	fresh parsley, finely chopped	30 mL
1 tsp	finely chopped fresh mint or lemon balm	5 mL
1	head of leaf lettuce	1
	salt and freshly ground black pepper, to taste	
	sugar, to taste	

• Heat the olive oil in a pan and cook the zucchinis until lightly browned all over, stirring occasionally. Sprinkle with dill.

• Pour the cooking liquid into a bowl and add the walnut oil, lemon juice, vinegar, pepper, salt and sugar. Mix well and set aside.

• Slice the tomatoes, slice the peppers into strips, then slice the onions into rings. Add the tomatoes, peppers and onions to the marinade and mix well.

• Add the zucchini slices, Feta and herbs to the marinade and mix all the ingredients together thoroughly.

• Cover and leave to marinate in the refrigerator for about 1 hour.

• Before serving, shred the lettuce leaves, then mix with the salad. Serve immediately.

Serving suggestions: Serve with ciabatta rolls or warmed pita bread.

Variations: Use red onions in place of standard onions. Use hazelnut or olive oil in place of walnut oil. Use other herb-flavored vinegars in place of tarragon vinegar. Use Cheddar or Mozzarella cheese in place of Feta cheese.

Cold Julienne of Vegetables with Apples

This delicious salad mixes cooked and raw vegetables in a tantalizing way.

Preparation time: 20 minutes · Cooking time: 10 minutes · Serves: 4

½ lb	green beans, pared	225 g
1	stick of celery, in julienne	1
2	carrots, peeled and pared, in julienne	2
1	yellow bell pepper, in julienne	1
1	orange bell pepper, in julienne	1
1	small cucumber, peeled, seeded, cut in thick julienne	1
14	mushrooms, cleaned and sliced	14
2	apples, cored, peeled and sliced	2
1 tsp	Dijon mustard	5 mL
⅓ cup	mayonnaise	75 mL
1 tbsp	sour cream	15 mL
¼ cup	toasted slivered almonds	60 mL
	salt and freshly ground black pepper	
	lemon juice	
	a few drops of Worcestershire sauce	
	cleaned mixed salad greens	
	chopped fresh parsley	

• Cook beans 5 minutes in salted, boiling water. Remove beans with slotted spoon and transfer to bowl of cold water. Add celery and carrots to boiling water; cook 4 minutes. Transfer to the bowl of cold water.

• Drain cooked vegetables and pat dry with paper towels.

• Placed cooked vegetables and raw peppers, cucumbers and mushrooms in large bowl. Add apples and season generously.

• In a separate bowl, mix mustard with mayonnaise and sour cream. Pour dressing over salad and mix well.

• Season with salt, pepper, lemon juice and Worcestershire sauce. Mix well.

• Line serving plates with mixed greens and top with vegetables. Sprinkle with toasted almonds and parsley. Serve.

●

Serving suggestions: Serve with thick slices of fresh multigrain or nut bread.

Variations: Use pears in place of the apples. Use slivers of walnut in place of almonds. Use low-fat plain yogurt in place of sour cream.

Kensington Salad

A satisfying main course salad for a summer lunch alfresco.

Preparation time: 10 minutes · Serves: 4

6	large mushrooms, thinly sliced	6
2	medium apples, cut into chunks and tossed in lemon juice	2
4	celery sticks, cut into matchstick strips	4
½ cup	walnut pieces	125 mL
2	bunches of watercress	2
DRESSING		
2 tbsp	mayonnaise	30 mL
2 tbsp	plain yogurt	30 mL
1 tsp	herb mustard	5 mL
	a little lemon juice	
	salt and freshly ground pepper	
	strawberry and kiwi slices, to garnish	

• Place the mushrooms, apple, celery and walnuts in a bowl.

• Combine all the ingredients for the dressing, pour over the vegetables and toss gently to mix.

• Arrange the watercress on a flat dish or platter and mound the salad mixture on top.

• Garnish with strawberry and kiwi slices and serve immediately.

Serving suggestion: Serve with warm ciabatta rolls.

Variations: A medium bulb of fennel, finely sliced, could be used in place of the celery. Use hazelnuts or almond flakes in place of walnuts. Use baby spinach leaves in place of watercress.

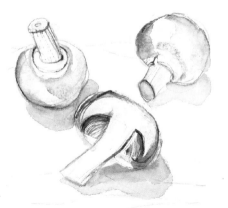

Mount Carmel Salad

Serve this crunchy salad as an accompaniment to a hot main dish or as a tasty snack.

Preparation time: 10 minutes · Serves: 4–6

2	medium carrots, peeled	2
1	green pepper	1
1–2	fresh apricots	1–2
1 tbsp	sesame seeds	15 mL
½ lb	bean sprouts	225 g
¼ cup	French (oil and vinegar) dressing	60 mL
2 tbsp	unsweetened pineapple juice	30 mL

• Cut the carrots into matchstick strips. Set aside.

• Seed and thinly slice the pepper. Set aside.

• Cut the apricots into slivers. Set aside.

• Toast the sesame seeds in a dry pan over a low heat until golden brown. Remove from the heat and set aside.

• Place the carrots, pepper, apricots and bean sprouts in a serving dish.

• Mix the French dressing with the pineapple juice in a bowl and fold into the salad.

• Sprinkle the sesame seeds over the top and serve at once.

Serving suggestions: Serve as an accompaniment to a vegetable flan or pizza, or with fresh crusty bread.

Variations: Use pumpkin or sunflower seeds in place of sesame seeds. Use apple or orange juice in place of pineapple juice. Use zucchinis in place of carrots.

COOK'S TIP

Use bean sprouts which are at least 1 in (2.5 cm) long for this recipe.

Mushroom Salad

This is an ideal way of enjoying the distinctive flavor of mushrooms. Use wild varieties combined with, or in place of cultivated ones when available.

Preparation time: 10 minutes, plus 1–2 hours chilling time · Cooking time: 5 minutes · Serves: 4–6

1 lb	button and/or oyster mushrooms, sliced thinly	450 g
1	medium onion, finely chopped	1
3 tbsp	vegetable oil	45 mL
1 tbsp	chopped fresh parsley	15 mL
1	cucumber, finely diced	1
3–4	tomatoes, skinned, seeded and sliced	3–4
4 tbsp	olive oil	60 mL
1 tbsp	white wine vinegar	15 mL
	freshly ground black pepper	
1	small head iceberg lettuce	1

• Heat the vegetable oil in a large frying pan. Gently cook the mushrooms and onion for 2–3 minutes, or until just soft, stirring. Set aside to cool.

• Stir the chopped parsley into the mushrooms with the cucumber and tomatoes.

• In a small bowl or jug, whisk together the olive oil, wine vinegar and pepper to taste with a fork, until thickened.

• Pour the dressing over the mushroom mixture and stir gently to coat. Chill the mushroom salad for 1–2 hours.

• Finely shred the lettuce and arrange on a serving plate. Spread the chilled mushroom salad over the lettuce and serve immediately.

Serving suggestions: Serve with melba toast or crusty wholewheat rolls.

Variations: Use chestnut mushrooms in place of button mushrooms. Use chantarelle or other wild mushrooms in place of oyster mushrooms. Use chopped fresh coriander in place of parsley.

COOK'S TIP

The salad can be prepared a day in advance and stored in the refrigerator until required.

Cucumber in a Creamy Dill Sauce

Fresh dill provides the perfect flavoring for cucumber in this unusual vegetable side dish.

Preparation time: 15 minutes · Cooking time: 20 minutes · Serves: 4–6

2–3	cucumbers, weighing about 1¾ lb (800 g) in total	2–3
1 tbsp	butter	15 mL
1	bunch of green onions, trimmed and sliced	1
1	red pepper, seeded and cut into small pieces	1
	finely grated rind and juice of 1 lemon	
	salt and white pepper	
8 tbsp	heavy cream	120 mL
2 tbsp	dry white wine	30 mL
1–2 tbsp	fresh dill, chopped	15–30 mL

• Remove and discard the skin from the cucumbers, then cut in half lengthwise. Remove and discard the seeds with a spoon and cut the flesh into slices about ½ in (1 cm) thick.

• Melt the butter in a pan, add the green onions and cook for 5 minutes, until softened, stirring occasionally.

• Add the cucumber and cook gently for 3 minutes, stirring occasionally.

• Add the pepper to the cucumber mixture and cook for 5 minutes, until softened, stirring occasionally.

• Add the lemon rind and juice and salt and pepper to taste. Cover the pan and cook gently for a further 7 minutes, stirring occasionally.

• Stir in the cream, then cook briefly over a higher heat before adding the wine.

• Sprinkle with chopped dill before serving. Serve hot.

Serving suggestions: Serve with cheese-topped baked potatoes and fresh crusty bread or grilled polenta.

Variations: Use fresh mint in place of dill. Use lime rind and juice in place of lemon. Use sour cream, or thick-set plain yogurt in place of cream.

Green Pepper Salad

Serve this salad in individual dishes as a starter accompanied by crusty brown bread or as a light lunch with bread and chunks of cheese.

Preparation time: 10 minutes, plus marinating time · Serves: 4–6

3	medium green peppers	3
3	medium tomatoes	3
2	medium onions	2
¾ cup	sprouted lentils	175 mL
	black grapes, to garnish	
DRESSING		
¼ cup	olive oil	60 mL
2 tbsp	red wine vinegar	30 mL
2 tsp	ground cumin	10 mL
½ tsp	chopped fresh coriander	2 mL

• Core, seed and thinly slice the peppers.

• Slice the tomatoes and onions.

• Arrange the peppers, tomatoes and onions alternately on a round serving dish and sprinkle the lentil sprouts over the top.

• In a bowl, whisk all the ingredients for the dressing together thoroughly and pour over the vegetables.

• Cover and leave to marinate for at least 1 hour at room temperature before serving.

• Just before serving, garnish with halved and seeded black grapes.

Serving suggestions: Serve with oven-baked potatoes with cheese or grilled polenta.

Variations: Use Italian plum tomatoes in place of standard tomatoes. Use alfalfa sprouts in place of sprouted lentils. Use walnut or hazelnut oil in place of olive oil. Use ground coriander in place of cumin.

COOK'S TIPS

Make sure you only sprout whole lentils – red split lentils will not sprout. You can prepare this salad in advance and refrigerate until required, but remove from the refrigerator 30 minutes before serving.

Bavarian Potato Salad

It is best to prepare this salad a few hours in advance to allow the potatoes time to absorb the delicious flavors.

Preparation time: 15 minutes · Cooking time: 15 minutes · Serves: 4–6

2 lbs	tiny new potatoes	1 kg
4 tbsp	olive oil	60 mL
4	green onions, finely chopped	4
2	cloves of garlic, crushed	2
2 tbsp	chopped fresh dill, or 2 tsp (10 mL) dried dill	30 mL
2 tbsp	wine vinegar	30 mL
½ tsp	sugar	2 mL
2 tbsp	fresh parsley, chopped	30 mL
	salt and freshly ground black pepper	

• Wash the potatoes but do not peel; place in a pan. Cover with water, bring to a boil and boil until just tender.

• Meanwhile, heat the oil in a frying pan and cook the green onions and garlic for 2–3 minutes, until they have softened a little, stirring frequently.

• Add the dill and cook gently for a further 1 minute.

• Add the wine vinegar and sugar and stir until the sugar melts. Remove from the heat and add a little salt and pepper.

• Drain the potatoes and pour over the dressing while they are still hot. Toss together to mix well.

• Allow to cool and sprinkle with the chopped parsley before serving.

Serving suggestion: Serve with oven-roasted or grilled fresh mixed vegetables.

Variations: Use 4 small shallots in place of green onions. Use mint in place of dill.

COOK'S TIP

Ready-prepared fresh garlic is available in jars, to save a little preparation time.

Mixed Pepper Salad

An impressive salad for entertaining friends. Grilling peppers under a broiler, or on the barbecue, gives them a deliciously smoky flavor.

Preparation time: 30 minutes, plus 1 hour chilling time · Cooking time: 5 minutes · Serves: 6–8

3	red peppers	3
3	green peppers	3
3	yellow peppers	3
2 tbsp	vegetable oil	30 mL
6 tbsp	sunflower oil	90 mL
2 tbsp	lemon juice	30 mL
2 tbsp	white wine vinegar	30 mL
1	small clove of garlic, crushed	1
	pinch of salt	
	pinch of cayenne pepper	
	pinch of sugar	
3	hard-boiled eggs	3
½ cup	black olives, pitted	125 mL
2 tbsp	fresh coriander leaves, finely chopped (optional)	30 mL

COOK'S TIP

The skinned peppers will keep in a refrigerator for up to 5 days if they are covered with a little oil.

• Cut the peppers in half, then remove and discard the cores and seeds. With the palm of your hand, lightly press the halved peppers down onto a flat surface to flatten out.

• Brush the skin side of each pepper with a little of the vegetable oil, then place under a preheated oven broiler. Cook until the skins begin to char and split.

• Remove the peppers from the grill and wrap them in a clean tea-towel or aluminum foil. Set aside for 10–15 minutes.

• Place the sunflower oil, lemon juice, wine vinegar, garlic, salt, cayenne and sugar in a small bowl and whisk together thoroughly with a fork, until thickened.

• Cut each hard-boiled egg into quarters.

• Unwrap the peppers and carefully peel away the skins. Cut the flesh into thick strips about 1 in (2.5 cm) wide.

• Arrange the pepper strips in a circle on a serving plate, alternating the colors.

• Arrange the olives and quartered eggs in the center.

• Sprinkle with coriander, if using, then spoon over the dressing.

• Chill the salad for at least 1 hour before serving.

Serving suggestions: Serve with crusty French bread or rolls.

Variations: Use walnut, hazelnut or olive oil in place of sunflower oil. Use tarragon vinegar in place of white wine vinegar. Use green olives in place of black olives.

Salad of Wild Mushrooms and Artichokes

Wild mushrooms are now readily available from supermarkets and grocery stores, and this recipe presents a delightful way of serving them.

Preparation time: 25 minutes · Cooking time: 12 minutes (microwave on HIGH) · Serves: 4

2	whole artichokes	2
2	slices of lemon	2
2	bay leaves	2
6	black peppercorns	6
2 cups	oyster mushrooms, or other varieties of wild mushroom	500 mL
2 tbsp	vegetable oil	30 mL
1	small head of radicchio	1
1	small head of iceberg lettuce	1
1	bunch of watercress	1
1	small bunch of fresh chives, snipped	1
6 tbsp	olive or peanut oil	90 mL
2 tbsp	white wine vinegar	30 mL
1 tbsp	Dijon mustard	15 mL
	salt and freshly ground black pepper	
	sprigs of fresh chervil or dill, to garnish	

• Trim the pointed tips from the artichoke leaves with scissors or a sharp knife. Place the trimmed artichokes into a microwave-proof bowl, along with the lemon, bay leaf, peppercorns and enough water to cover.

• Cook in a microwave oven on HIGH for 7–8 minutes, or until one of the bottom leaves pulls away easily. Stand the artichokes upside-down on a wire rack to drain completely and set aside.

• Remove and discard the stalks from the mushrooms and thickly slice the caps.

• Place the mushroom slices in a bowl with the vegetable oil and stir to coat each slice with a little of the oil. Cook on HIGH for 1–2 minutes. Set the mushrooms aside.

• Tear the radicchio and lettuce leaves into small pieces and place them in a bowl. Remove the leaves from the watercress and add these to the lettuce in the bowl along with the snipped chives.

• In a small bowl, whisk together the oil, wine vinegar, mustard and salt and pepper using a fork or a small whisk. Continue whisking until the dressing is thick and pale in color. Set aside.

• Remove the leaves from the drained artichokes and arrange attractively on 4 serving plates. Arrange the leaf salad over the artichoke leaves.

• Cut away and discard the fluffy choke from the artichoke hearts. Trim the artichoke hearts and cut into thin slices. Add the hearts to the bowl of sliced mushrooms and stir well. Pour half of the prepared dressing over the mushrooms and the artichoke hearts and toss to mix well.

• Spoon equal amounts of the mushroom mixture over the leaves and salad on the plates.

• Reheat each serving for 1 minute on HIGH, garnish with the chervil or dill and serve the remaining dressing separately.

●

Serving suggestion: Serve with warmed or toasted pita bread.

Asparagus Salad

A delightful way to enjoy fresh, tender asparagus spears.

Preparation time: 20–25 minutes · Cooking time: 10–15 minutes · Serves: 4

1½ lb	fresh asparagus	750 g
16	radishes	16
¾ lb	cherry tomatoes	340 g
¾ lb	small potatoes, peeled and cooked	340 g
8	green onions	8
DRESSING		
½ cup	garlic oil	120 mL
5 tbsp	herb vinegar	80 mL
1 tsp	mild mustard	5 mL
	salt and freshly ground black pepper	
	green onion leaves or chives, partly chopped, to garnish	

• Discard any woody ends from the asparagus and peel the stems. Bring a large pan of salted water to a boil, then cook the asparagus for about 10–15 minutes, until tender.

• Remove the asparagus, drain well, then slice into pieces about 2 in (5 cm) long. Set aside.

• Trim and slice the radishes. Remove and discard the stalks and cores from the tomatoes, then cut into slices.

• Cut the potatoes into slices. Trim the green onions, then cut into thin slices.

• In a bowl, mix the asparagus, radishes, tomatoes, potatoes and green onions together.

• For the dressing, whisk the oil, vinegar and mustard together in a bowl and season with salt and pepper to taste.

• Add the dressing to the vegetable salad, gently mix together thoroughly and set aside for 30 minutes before serving, to allow the flavors to mingle.

• Serve, garnished with the green onion leaves or chives.

●

Serving suggestions: Serve with crusty French bread or Italian ciabatta rolls.

Variations: Use baby plum tomatoes in place of cherry tomatoes. Use walnut or hazelnut oil or olive oil in place of garlic oil. Use baby corn in place of asparagus.

Spanish Salad
A vibrant and versatile mixed salad.

Preparation time: 15 minutes · Serves: 4–6

5	tomatoes	5
1	cucumber	1
3	green peppers	3
2–3	red onions	2–3
1	head of leaf lettuce, leaves separated	1
1	hard-boiled egg, sliced, to garnish	
	stuffed olives, to garnish	
DRESSING		
3 tbsp	olive oil	45 mL
4 tbsp	wine vinegar	60 mL
1 tbsp	fresh parsley, chopped	15 mL
1 tbsp	fresh chives, chopped	15 mL
	salt and freshly ground black pepper	
	sugar	

• Slice the tomatoes and cucumber and place in a salad bowl.

• Cut the peppers in half lengthwise. Remove and discard the cores and seeds, then slice the flesh into thin strips. Add to the salad bowl.

• Slice the onions and separate the rings. Add to the salad bowl.

• Tear the lettuce leaves into pieces and add to the bowl. Toss the salad ingredients to mix.

• For the dressing, in a small bowl, whisk together the oil, wine vinegar, 1 tbsp (15 mL) water and chopped herbs with a fork, until thickened. Season to taste with salt and pepper and a little sugar.

• Pour the dressing over the salad and toss thoroughly to coat.

• Garnish the salad with the hard-boiled egg slices and olives before serving.

Serving suggestions: Serve as an accompaniment to stuffed peppers or grilled or barbecued fish.

Variations: Use 2 medium-sized dill pickles in place of the fresh cucumber. Use plum tomatoes in place of ordinary tomatoes. Add some finely chopped anchovy fillets or canned, drained tuna for a tasty change.

Green and Gold Sunflower Salad

This colorful salad makes a spectacular and delicious addition to a summer meal.

Preparation time: 15 minutes · Serves: 4

3 tbsp	sunflower oil	45 mL
1 tbsp	lemon juice	15 mL
2	large ripe avocados	2
8	ripe apricots	8
6 tbsp	plain yogurt	150 mL
2 tsp	honey	10 mL
	grated rind of 1 lemon	
2 tsp	chopped fresh parsley	10 mL
1	small butterhead (or Boston) lettuce, separated into leaves	1
½ cup	toasted sunflower seeds	125 mL
	salt and freshly ground black pepper	

• Place the oil and lemon juice in a bowl and season with salt and pepper. Mix together thoroughly.

• Cut the avocados in half lengthwise, then remove and discard the pits. Peel, then cut into neat slices.

• Mix the avocado slices with the oil and lemon juice very carefully, taking care not to break them up.

• Cut the apricots in half, then remove and discard the pits. If the apricots are large, cut in half again. Add to the avocados in the dressing.

• In another bowl, mix together the yogurt, honey, lemon rind and parsley.

• Divide the lettuce leaves between 4 individual serving plates and arrange the avocado and apricots on top in a sunflower design.

• Spoon a little of the yogurt mixture over the salad, then sprinkle with sunflower seeds. Pour any remaining yogurt dressing into a small jug and serve separately.

Serving suggestions: Serve as an appetizer or as an accompaniment to a chicken or fish dish.

Variations: Use segments of ruby grapefruit or peaches in place of apricots. Use pine nuts in place of sunflower seeds.

Cucumber and Pineapple Salad

This is a refreshing salad to accompany a light, summer meal.

Preparation time: 10 minutes, plus 30 minutes soaking time · Serves: 4

4 tsp	raisins	20 mL
¼ cup	pineapple juice	60 mL
1	medium cucumber	1
1	large red pepper	1
2 cups	pineapple chunks	500 mL
¼ cup	oil and vinegar (French) dressing	60 mL
1 tsp	fresh mint, finely chopped	5 mL
2 tsp	sesame seeds	10 mL

• Soak the raisins in the pineapple juice in a bowl for at least ½ hour.

• Thinly slice the cucumber.

• Seed the pepper and finely chop.

• If using fresh pineapple, chop into cubes.

• Arrange the cucumber on a serving plate.

• Mix the pepper, pineapple and soaked raisins together and pile into the center of the cucumber.

• Mix the dressing and mint together and pour over the salad just before serving.

• Sprinkle the sesame seeds over the top and serve immediately.

●

Serving suggestions: Serve with vegetable quiche and vegetable roasts for a main course, or with crusty bread for a light meal.

Variations: Use orange or apple juice in place of pineapple juice. Use sunflower seeds in place of sesame seeds.

COOK'S TIP

●

Canned pineapple (in fruit juice, preferably without sugar added) can be used if fresh pineapple is not available.

Hearty Salads

Pasta and Asparagus Salad

This elegant green salad is a wonderful way of making the most of fresh asparagus.

Preparation time: 15 minutes · Cooking time: 15 minutes · Serves: 4

4 oz	fettucine	115 g
1 lb	asparagus, trimmed and cut into 1-in (2.5-cm) pieces	450 g
2	zucchinis, cut into 2-in (5-cm) sticks	2
2 tbsp	fresh parsley, chopped	30 mL
2 tbsp	fresh marjoram, chopped	30 mL
1	lemon, peeled and segmented	1
6 tbsp	olive oil	90 mL
1	head of crisp or iceberg lettuce	1
1	head of endive or frisée lettuce	1
	salt and freshly ground black pepper	
	grated rind and juice of 1 lemon	
	pinch of sugar (optional)	

COOK'S TIP

Place the ingredients for the lemon dressing in a clean screw-top jar and shake vigorously to blend thoroughly.

• Place the pasta in a saucepan and cover with boiling water. Season with a little salt and simmer for 10–12 minutes, until just cooked or al dente. Rinse the pasta under cold water, then set aside to cool completely.

• Cook the asparagus and zucchinis in a saucepan of boiling water for 3–5 minutes, until just cooked and tender.

• Drain the asparagus and zucchinis into a colander and rinse them in cold water to refresh.

• Place the pasta, cooked vegetables, herbs and lemon segments in a large bowl and mix them together carefully to avoid breaking up the vegetables.

• In a separate bowl, mix together the lemon rind and juice, oil, sugar, if using, and salt and pepper.

• Pour the lemon and oil dressing over the pasta mixture in the bowl and mix well to coat the vegetables and pasta evenly.

• Arrange the lettuce and endive lettuce on serving plates and pile equal quantities of the asparagus and pasta mixture onto each plate. Serve.

Serving suggestion: Serve with thick slices of wholewheat bread.

Variations: Use mushrooms in place of asparagus. Use oranges in place of lemons. Use spaghetti in place of fettucine.

Gianfottere Salad

This interesting Italian-style dish makes the most of delicious summer vegetables.

Preparation time: 30 minutes, plus 30 minutes standing time · Cooking time: 30 minutes · Serves: 4

1	small eggplant	1
2	tomatoes	2
1	large zucchini	1
1	red pepper	1
1	green pepper	1
1	medium onion	1
1	clove of garlic	1
4 tbsp	olive oil	60 mL
1 lb	wholewheat pasta spirals or bows	450 g
	freshly ground sea salt and black pepper	

• Cut the eggplant into ½-in (1-cm) slices and place in a colander. Sprinkle with salt and leave to drain for 30 minutes.

• Remove and discard the hard cores from the tomatoes and roughly chop the flesh.

• Cut the zucchini into ½-in (1-cm) slices.

• Core and seed the peppers, then roughly chop.

• Chop the onion and crush the garlic.

• Heat 3 tbsp (45 mL) of the oil in a frying pan and cook the onion gently until transparent but not colored, stirring occasionally.

• Rinse the salt from the eggplant thoroughly and pat dry with absorbent kitchen paper. Roughly chop the eggplant.

• Stir the eggplant, zucchini, peppers, tomatoes and garlic into the onion and cook gently for 20 minutes, stirring occasionally. Season with salt and pepper to taste and set aside to cool completely.

• Cook the pasta in a pan of boiling salted water for 10–15 minutes, until just tender or al dente.

• Rinse the pasta in cold water and drain well.

• Place the pasta in a large mixing bowl and stir in the remaining 1 tbsp (15 mL) oil.

• Stir the vegetables into the cooked pasta, mixing well to ensure that they are evenly distributed.

Serving suggestions: Serve with warmed ciabatta Italian rolls, or as an accompaniment to fish or egg dishes.

Variations: Use sliced mushrooms in place of eggplants – there is no need to salt them. Use 1 leek in place of the onion. Use mixed red and green pasta shapes in place of wholewheat pasta.

Pasta, Pea and Pepper Salad

This highly colorful salad is simple to make but substantial enough to be served as a meal in itself.

Preparation time: 20 minutes · Cooking time: 15 minutes · Serves: 4

8 oz	plain and wholewheat pasta shells, mixed	230 g
2 cups	frozen peas	500 mL
2	small green peppers, seeded and sliced	2
2	small red peppers, seeded and sliced	2
2	small yellow peppers, seeded and sliced	2
½ cup	vegetable or olive oil	125 mL
¼ cup	white wine vinegar	60 mL
1 tbsp	Dijon or whole-grain mustard	15 mL
2 tsp	poppy seeds	10 mL
2 tsp	fresh parsley, chopped	10 mL
1 tsp	fresh thyme, chopped	5 mL
4	green onions, shredded	4
1 cup	Cheddar cheese, finely grated	250 mL
	mixed salad leaves, to serve	
	salt and freshly ground black pepper	

• Cook the pasta in a large saucepan of lightly salted, boiling water for 8–10 minutes, until cooked or al dente. Drain well and set aside.

• Cook the peas and the sliced peppers in a pan of lightly salted, boiling water for 3 minutes. Drain and set aside to cool.

• Place the oil, wine vinegar, mustard, poppy seeds, herbs and a little salt and pepper in a bowl.

• Using a fork or small whisk, whisk the dressing ingredients together vigorously, until the dressing is thick and pale in color.

• Place the pasta in a large bowl and stir in the cooked vegetables.

• Pour the dressing over the pasta and vegetables and toss together thoroughly to coat the ingredients completely. Cover and chill the pasta salad in the refrigerator before serving.

• Stir the green onions and cheese into the pasta salad and serve immediately on a bed of mixed salad leaves.

Serving suggestion: Serve with wedges of focaccia or slices of ciabatta.

Variations: Use ½ cup (125 mL) salted peanuts in place of the cheese. Use frozen baby broad beans in place of peas.

Multicolored Pasta Salad

An attractive pasta salad with mixed vegetables and a mayonnaise dressing.

Preparation time: 15 minutes · Cooking time: 20 minutes · Serves: 4

8 oz	farfalle or pasta bows	225 g
3	medium carrots, sliced	3
1 cup	cauliflower, broken into florets	250 mL
1 cup	frozen peas	250 mL
½–¾ cup	mayonnaise	125–175 mL
4	hard-boiled eggs, quartered	4
	fresh herb sprigs, to garnish	

• Cook the pasta in a pan of boiling water for 8–10 minutes, until just cooked or al dente.

• Rinse, drain thoroughly and set aside to cool.

• Meanwhile, cook the carrots in a pan of boiling water, covered, for about 5 minutes, then add the cauliflower and cook for 4 minutes.

• Add the peas and cook for a further 1–2 minutes, until cooked.

• Drain the vegetables and set aside to cool.

• Once cool, place the vegetables in a bowl with the pasta and mix well.

• Add the mayonnaise and toss to mix, then add the hard-boiled egg quarters and carefully mix again. Serve, garnished with fresh herb sprigs.

Serving suggestions: Serve with fresh crusty French bread or Italian ciabatta rolls.

Variations: Use broccoli in place of cauliflower. Use a yogurt dressing in place of mayonnaise for a reduced-fat alternative. Use corn in place of peas.

Rice and Nut Salad

This refreshing salad is healthy and nutritious, being high in protein and very low in saturated fats.

Preparation time: 15 minutes, plus standing time · Serves: 4

2 tbsp	olive oil	30 mL
2 tbsp	lemon juice	30 mL
⅔ cup	sultana raisins	150 mL
⅓ cup	currants	75 mL
1⅔ cups	cooked brown rice, well drained	400 mL
¾ cup	blanched almonds, chopped	175 mL
½ cup	cashew nuts, chopped	125 mL
½ cup	shelled walnuts, chopped	125 mL
1	14-oz(398-mL) can of peach slices in natural juice, drained and chopped	1
¼	cucumber, cubed	¼
½ cup	cooked red kidney beans	125 mL
1 tbsp	pitted black olives	15 mL
	freshly ground sea salt and black pepper	
	mixed salad leaves, to serve	

• Place the oil, lemon juice and salt and pepper to taste in a screw-top jar. Shake vigorously until the mixture has thickened. Set aside.

• Place the sultana raisins and currants in a small bowl and cover with boiling water. Allow to stand for 10 minutes before draining the fruit.

• Mix together the rice, nuts, soaked fruit, peaches, cucumber, beans and olives in a large mixing bowl.

• Pour the dressing over the salad and mix together thoroughly, to ensure all the ingredients are evenly coated. Serve on a bed of mixed salad leaves.

Serving suggestions: Serve with herb-flavored bread, or with plain grilled chicken or fish.

Variations: Use canned apricots in place of peaches. Use pecan nuts in place of cashew nuts. Use hazelnuts in place of almonds. Use cooked flageolet or black-eyed beans in place of red kidney beans.

Caribbean Rice and Beans

This dish, originally from Cuba, is also called Moors and Christians because of the use of black beans and white rice.

Preparation time: 10 minutes · Cooking time: 1–1½ hours for the beans; 25–30 minutes for the finished dish · Serves: 4

1 cup	black beans, soaked overnight and cooked until soft	250 mL
3 tbsp	vegetable oil	45 mL
2	small onions, chopped	2
4	cloves of garlic, crushed	4
2	small green peppers, seeded and finely chopped	2
4	tomatoes, skinned and finely chopped	4
1¼ cups	long-grain rice	300 mL
	salt and freshly ground black pepper	
	fresh herb sprigs, to garnish	

• Drain the cooked beans and mash ¼ cup (60 mL) to a paste with a fork, adding a little water if necessary. Set aside.

• Heat the oil in a pan and fry the onions, garlic and peppers until soft, stirring occasionally.

• Add the tomato and cook for a further 2 minutes.

• Add the bean paste and stir into mix.

• Add the remaining cooked beans and rice, and enough water to cover.

• Bring to a boil, cover and simmer for 20–25 minutes, until the rice is just cooked or al dente, stirring occasionally.

• Season to taste with salt and pepper, and serve hot, garnished with sprigs of fresh herbs.

Serving suggestion: Serve with a crisp green salad and crusty bread.

Variations: Use other beans such as flageolet or butter beans in place of black beans. Use 1 baby leek in place of onion.

Leila's Salad

Cooked rice and raw fresh vegetables are tossed together in a flavorful dressing to create an appealing light lunch.

Preparation time: 15 minutes · Serves: 4

1⅓ cup	long-grain brown rice, cooked and cooled	325 mL
¾ cup	prepared pineapple, diced	175 mL
8	green onions, finely chopped	8
½ cup	almond flakes, lightly toasted	125 mL
8	radishes, thinly sliced	8
1½ cups	bean sprouts	350 mL
	twists of lime, to garnish	

DRESSING

3 tbsp	sunflower or safflower oil	45 mL
1 tbsp	sherry	15 mL
	juice of 1 lime	
1 tsp	grated ginger	5 mL
	salt and freshly ground black pepper	

• In a bowl, combine the rice with the pineapple, green onions, almonds, radishes and bean sprouts. Set aside.

• In a small bowl, combine all the dressing ingredients until thoroughly mixed.

• Pour the dressing over the salad and gently toss together to mix.

• Cover and refrigerate until required.

• Garnish with twists of lime and serve.

Serving suggestions: Serve with stuffed pancakes or fresh crusty bread.

Variations: Use sprouted chickpeas in place of bean sprouts. Use chopped hazelnuts or walnuts in place of almonds. Use mango in place of pineapple.

COOK'S TIP

Use prepared root ginger, available in jars, to save a little preparation time.

Broccoli and Cauliflower Salad

A simple, crisp vegetable salad served with a creamy plain yogurt dressing.

Preparation time: 10 minutes · Serves: 4

1	red pepper	1
1	small head of broccoli	1
1	small head of cauliflower	1
1 tbsp	toasted almond flakes	15 mL
DRESSING		
¼ cup	plain yogurt	60 mL
2 tbsp	fresh lemon juice	30 mL
2 tbsp	olive oil	30 mL
	salt and freshly ground black pepper	
	pinch of ground nutmeg	

• Seed the pepper and cut into matchstick pieces. Set aside.

• Trim the broccoli and cauliflower and break into small florets.

• Place the pepper, broccoli and cauliflower in a mixing bowl.

• For the dressing, combine the yogurt, lemon juice, oil, salt and pepper and nutmeg in a clean screw-top jar and shake well.

• Pour the dressing over the salad and toss together to mix well.

• Divide the mixture between 4 individual serving plates or bowls and garnish with the almond flakes. Serve.

●

Serving suggestions: Serve with crackers, oatcakes or crusty fresh bread.

Variations: Omit the nutmeg from the dressing and add a few chopped fresh herbs. Use 3 cups (750 mL) cherry tomatoes or button mushrooms in place of cauliflower. Use fresh lime juice in place of lemon juice.

Tabouleh

This traditional Middle-Eastern dish is delicious yet quick and easy to make.

Preparation time: 15 minutes, plus 1 hour standing time · Serves: 4

1 cup	cooked couscous	250 mL
4	medium tomatoes, finely chopped	4
3 cups	cucumber, finely chopped	750 mL
4	shallots, thinly sliced	4
	salt and freshly ground black pepper	
	juice of 2 lemons	
	finely grated rind of 2 lemons	
1½ tbsp	finely chopped, fresh flat-leaf parsley	25 mL
1½ tbsp	finely chopped fresh mint	25 mL
	lemon slices and fresh herb sprigs, to garnish	

• Rinse the couscous under running cold water in a very fine sieve. Place in a bowl.

• Add the tomato, cucumber, shallot, salt and pepper to taste, lemon juice and lemon rind.

• Stir the mixture together well, cover and set aside in a refrigerator for 1–2 hours.

• Add the chopped herbs to the couscous mixture, taste and adjust the seasoning.

• Serve, garnished with the lemon slices and fresh herb sprigs.

Serving suggestion: Serve on a bed of lettuce with a poached egg on top.

Variations: Use cooked, prepared bulgur wheat in place of couscous. Use lime juice and rind in place of lemon. Use mushrooms or radishes in place of cucumber.

Flageolet Fiesta
A herb-flavored bean dish to delight the tastebuds.

Preparation time: 15 minutes, plus 2 hours marinating time · Cooking time: 1 hour · Serves: 4

1 cup	flageolet beans, soaked overnight and drained	250 mL
1	medium onions	1
2	cloves of garlic	2
½	cucumber	½
2 tbsp	chopped fresh parsley	30 mL
2 tbsp	chopped fresh mint	30 mL
2 tbsp	olive oil	30 mL
	juice and grated rind of 1 lemon	
	salt and freshly ground black pepper	
	watercress, to garnish	

• Cook the flageolet beans in a saucepan in plenty of boiling water for about 1 hour, or until just tender.

• Drain, place in a mixing bowl and set aside.

• Peel and finely chop the onions. Crush the garlic and chop the cucumber into bite-sized pieces.

• Add the onion, garlic, cucumber, herbs, oil, lemon juice and rind to the beans and mix well.

• Add salt and pepper to taste, cover and put in refrigerator to marinate for 2 hours.

• Transfer to a clean serving bowl and serve garnished with watercress.

Serving suggestion: Serve with slices of crusty French bread.

Variations: Use red kidney beans in place of flageolet beans. Use flavored oil such as chili or herb oil in place of olive oil. Use lime rind and juice in place of lemon.

Butter Bean, Lemon and Fennel Salad

This interesting salad makes an unusual lunch or supper dish.

Preparation time: 15 minutes, plus standing time · Cooking time: 1 hour 20 minutes (microwave) · Serves: 4

1 cup	dried butter beans	250 mL
2	small bulbs of fennel, thinly sliced (keep leaves for the dressing)	2
4	lemons	4
¼ cup	vegetable oil	60 mL
	large pinch of sugar	
	salt and freshly ground black pepper	
	lettuce and radicchio leaves, for serving	
	fresh herb sprigs, to garnish	

• Place the beans in a bowl and cover completely with cold water. Cook in a microwave oven on HIGH for 10 minutes, then remove and allow to stand for 1 hour.

• Drain the beans and discard the cooking liquid. Return the beans to the bowl and cover with fresh water.

• Cook the beans on MEDIUM for 1 hour. Leave to stand for 10 minutes before draining thoroughly.

• Place 2¼ cups (600 mL) water in a bowl and bring to boil, cooking on HIGH for 5–7 minutes.

• Blanch the fennel slices in the boiling water for 2 minutes on HIGH. Drain the fennel thoroughly and set aside.

• Remove the rind from the lemons using a potato peeler. Make sure to remove any white pith from the rind.

• Cut the rind into very thin strips and set aside for garnishing.

• Squeeze the juice from the lemons. Place 2½ tbsp (40 mL) lemon juice, the oil, sugar and salt and pepper to taste in a small bowl and whisk together with a fork or small whisk until the mixture is thick.

• Finely chop the reserved fennel leaves and add to the dressing.

• Mix the cooked beans and fennel together in a bowl.

• Pour over the lemon dressing and mix well to coat all the ingredients thoroughly.

• Serve on a bed of mixed lettuce and radicchio. Garnish with fresh herb sprigs and the reserved lemon rind.

●

Serving suggestions: Serve with boiled new potatoes in their skins or baked potatoes.

Variations: Use other dried beans such as flageolet or black-eyed beans in place of butter beans. Use lime rind and juice in place of lemon. Use walnut or hazelnut oil for a tasty variation.

Salade de Légumes

This salad is simplicity itself to prepare yet special enough for a dinner party. It is best served warm.

Preparation time: 15 minutes · Cooking time: 2–6 minutes (microwave on HIGH) · Serves: 6

9–10 oz	canned artichoke hearts	250–280 g
1	red onion, chopped or 4 green onions, thinly sliced	1
1	clove of garlic, crushed	1
1	green pepper, seeded and chopped	1
1 tsp	chopped fresh basil	5 mL
1 tsp	chopped fresh thyme	5 mL
2 tsp	chopped fresh parsley	10 mL
3 cups	cooked or canned haricot beans, white kidney beans, or butter beans, rinsed and drained	750 mL
4	tomatoes, skinned, seeded and chopped	4
1	head each of radicchio and curly endive	1

DRESSING

3 tbsp	olive oil	45 mL
2 tbsp	white wine vinegar	30 mL
½ tsp	Dijon mustard	2 mL
	pinch of salt and freshly ground black pepper	

• Place artichoke hearts in a large microwave-proof casserole dish. Stir in the remaining ingredients, except the dressing and salad leaves, and heat on HIGH for 2 minutes to warm through.

• Place the dressing ingredients in a small bowl and whisk together with a fork, until thickened. Pour over the warm salad and toss to coat.

• Arrange the radicchio and endive leaves on individual serving plates. Pile the salad on top.

• Spoon over any excess dressing and serve immediately.

Serving suggestion: Serve as a starter or a light main course with wholewheat toast.

Variations: Use red pepper in place of green pepper. Add drained, canned tuna or salmon to the salad, if you like.

COOK'S TIP

Mix the dressing into the warm ingredients immediately to bring out their flavors.

Marinated Beans

These dressed beans make a substantial vegetarian starter.

Preparation time: 15 minutes, plus soaking and marinating time · Cooking time: 1½ hours · Serves: 4

1 cup	mixed brown and white beans	250 mL
1	sprig of fresh thyme	1
2 cups	vegetable stock	500 mL
2	whole cloves	2
1	onion	1
2	cloves of garlic	2
1	bay leaf	1
	fresh herb sprigs, to garnish	

DRESSING

1	onion, sliced	1
	sea salt, to sprinkle	
2	cloves of garlic, crushed	2
½–1 tsp	Dijon mustard	2.5 mL–5 mL
½–1 tsp	dried oregano	2.5 mL–5 mL
4 tbsp	red wine vinegar	60 mL
5 tbsp	olive oil	75 mL
1	bunch of fresh parsley, finely chopped	
	freshly ground black pepper, to taste	

• Wash the beans and place in a bowl. Cover with water, add the thyme sprig and leave to soak overnight. Drain.

• Pour the stock into a pan and add the beans.

• Press the cloves into the peeled onion, then add the onion, garlic and bay leaf to the stock and beans. Stir to mix.

• Bring to a boil, then cover, reduce the heat and simmer for 1½ hours, until the beans are cooked and tender, stirring occasionally.

• Strain through a sieve or colander and reserve the beans. Discard the stock, onion and garlic.

• Meanwhile, for the dressing, place the onion in a bowl and sprinkle with sea salt.

• Leave for 10 minutes to allow the salt to be absorbed.

• Add the crushed garlic to the onion with the mustard, oregano, wine vinegar, oil, parsley and pepper to taste.

• Mix the dressing with the beans, cover and leave to marinate in the refrigerator for several hours before serving. Serve, garnished with fresh herb sprigs.

●

Serving suggestion: Serve with garlic bread.

Variations: Use wholegrain mustard in place of Dijon mustard. Use walnut or hazelnut oil in place of olive oil. Use fresh basil in place of parsley

Bean Salad

A classic mixed-bean salad for a colorful and flavorful main course.

Preparation time: 10 minutes, plus 30 minutes standing time · Cooking time: 3–4 minutes · Serves: 4

1 lb	green beans	450 g
1	14-oz (398-mL) can of red kidney beans, drained	1
1	14-oz (398-mL) can of haricot beans (or white kidney beans), drained	1
DRESSING		
3 tbsp	salad oil	45 mL
1–2 tbsp	wine vinegar	15–30 mL
	salt and freshly ground black pepper	
	sugar	
1 tbsp	chopped mixed herbs	15 mL
1	onion, finely chopped	1

• Trim the green beans and cut into shorter lengths. Cook in a pan of salted boiling water for about 3–4 minutes, until just tender. Drain thoroughly and set aside.

• For the dressing, in a bowl, whisk together the oil, wine vinegar and salt and pepper and sugar to taste with a fork, until thickened.

• Add the chopped herbs and onion to the dressing and mix well.

• Mix the warm green beans with the drained canned beans in a serving dish. Pour over the dressing and toss thoroughly to coat.

• Allow the salad to stand for at least 30 minutes before serving.

Serving suggestion: Serve as a main course salad with fresh crusty bread.

Variations: Use fresh broad beans in place of green beans. Use canned flageolet or butter beans in place of the haricot beans. Use herb vinegar for extra flavor, or use lemon juice in place of vinegar.

Black-Eyed Beans and Orange Salad

This appetizing salad has a delightfully fresh taste which is given 'bite' by the addition of watercress.

Preparation time: 20 minutes, plus standing time · Cooking time: 1 hour 10–12 minutes (microwave) · Serves: 4

1 cup	dried black-eyed beans	250 mL
4	bay leaves	4
4	slices of onion	4
	juice and grated rind of 2 small oranges	
4 tbsp	olive or grapeseed oil	60 mL
8	black olives, pitted and quartered	8
4	green onions, chopped	4
2½ tbsp	chopped fresh parsley	40 mL
2½ tbsp	chopped fresh basil leaves	40 mL
	salt and freshly ground black pepper	
4	whole oranges	4
	watercress, to serve	

• Place the beans in a microwave-proof bowl and cover with cold water.

• Cook in microwave on HIGH for 10–12 minutes; allow to stand for 1 hour, then drain the beans and discard the cooking liquid.

• Return the beans to the bowl and re-cover with fresh water. Add the bay leaves and onion slices.

• Cover the bowl with plastic wrap and pierce several times with the tip of a sharp knife. Cook on MEDIUM for 1 hour, then stand for 10 minutes before draining thoroughly. Discard the bay leaf and onion.

• Place the orange juice, rind and oil in a bowl and whisk with a fork.

• Stir the olives, green onions and chopped herbs into the orange and oil dressing.

• Add the cooked, drained beans to the dressing mixture in the bowl, season to taste with salt and pepper and mix thoroughly to coat the beans well.

• Carefully peel the oranges; remove as much white pith as possible.

• Cut the oranges into segments, removing and discarding the thin inner membrane and any remaining white pith from each segment.

• Reserve 4 to 6 orange segments and chop the remaining segments. Mix these chopped segments into the bean salad.

• Arrange the watercress on a serving plate and top with the bean and orange salad.

• Arrange the remaining orange slices on the plate for garnish and serve immediately.

Serving suggestions: Serve in split wholewheat pita bread or in taco shells.

Variations: Use 1 stick of celery in place of green onion. Use walnut or hazelnut oil in place of olive oil. Use fresh chives in place of basil.

Soups

Rasam

This spicy lentil soup is a traditional southern Indian favorite.

Preparation time: 20 minutes · Cooking time: 15 minutes · Serves: 4

1 tbsp	vegetable oil	15 mL
1 tsp	mustard seeds	5 mL
5	whole red chilies	5
10	curry leaves	10
	pinch of asafetida	
2 tbsp	crushed garlic	30 mL
1 tsp	ground turmeric	5 mL
½ cup	split red lentils, washed and cleaned	125 mL
2–3	tomatoes, skinned and quartered	2–3
3–4	black peppercorns	3–4
1	green chili, seeded and sliced	3
3½ oz	tamarind pulp	100 g
	salt, to taste	

• Heat the oil in a saucepan. Add the mustard seeds and cook until they begin to crackle. Add the whole red chilies, curry leaves, asafetida and crushed garlic. Stir for a few seconds.

• Add the turmeric, lentils, tomatoes, peppercorns, green chili, tamarind pulp and salt. Stir and add approximately 4 cups (1 litre) water.

• Bring to a boil and simmer gently until the lentils are cooked and soft, stirring occasionally.

Vegetable Soup with Sprouts

A nutritious soup for a satisfying supper or lunch.

Preparation time: 10 minutes · Cooking time: 20 minutes · Serves: 4

4 tsp	olive oil	20 mL
2	cloves of garlic, crushed	2
2	red peppers, seeded and sliced	2
½–¾ cup	canned haricot beans (or navy beans), drained	120–180 mL
3½ cups	vegetable stock	800 mL
2 tsp	paprika	10 mL
4	handfuls vegetable sprouts, such as alfalfa or cress	4
4	fresh herb sprigs, to garnish	4

• Heat the oil in a saucepan and add the garlic. Cook briefly, stirring.

• Add the peppers and cook for 4–5 minutes, stirring occasionally.

• Add the beans and stock to the pan with the paprika and mix well.

• Bring to a boil, cover and cook gently for 10 minutes, stirring occasionally.

• Add the vegetable sprouts to the pan and stir. Allow to cook very briefly, then adjust the seasoning.

• Serve the soup immediately in a warmed soup bowl, garnished with a fresh herb sprig.

Serving suggestion: Serve with wholewheat or multigrain rolls.

Variations: Use canned red kidney beans or chickpeas in place of haricot beans. Use yellow or green pepper in place of red. Use a little grated fresh root ginger in place of garlic.

Rasam

Daal Soup

Thick, hearty and slightly spicy, this soup can be made with either red or yellow lentils.

Preparation time: 15–20 minutes · Cooking time: 15 minutes · Serves: 6

1½ cups	red or yellow lentils	325 mL
4 cups	water or stock	1 L
4	canned tomatoes, drained and crushed	4
1	green chili, sliced lengthwise and seeded	1
2 tbsp	plain yogurt or sour cream	30 mL
1 tbsp	butter	15 mL
	salt and freshly ground black pepper	
1	medium onion, chopped or sliced into rings	1
1–2	sprigs fresh coriander, chopped	1–2

• Wash the lentils in 4–5 changes of water. Drain well and place in a large saucepan with the water or stock.

• Cover the pan and bring to a boil over a moderate heat. Reduce the heat and simmer for about 10–15 minutes, or until the lentils are soft. Add extra water if necessary.

• Remove the pan from the heat. Using a balloon whisk, beat the lentils until smooth.

• Return the pan to the heat, add the tomatoes and chili and simmer for 2 minutes.

• Remove the pan from the heat and allow to cool slightly, then beat in the yogurt or sour cream. Gently reheat the soup, stirring frequently, but do not allow to boil. Season with salt and pepper.

• Melt the butter in a small pan and fry the onions over a low heat, stirring, until softened but not colored.

• Remove and discard the chili from the soup, then pour the soup into warmed serving bowls. Sprinkle over the chopped coriander and fried onion and serve immediately.

Serving suggestion: Serve with slices of buttered wholewheat bread or warmed crusty rolls.

Variations: Use fresh plum tomatoes, skinned, in place of canned tomatoes.

COOK'S TIP

The cooked lentils can be puréed in a food processor or blender.

Creamed Corn Soup

Mixed Vegetable and Barley Soup

Creamed Corn Soup

Serve this luxurious soup with fresh crusty French or Italian bread.

Preparation time: 10 minutes · Cooking time: 25–30 minutes · Serves: 4–6

2 tbsp	olive oil	30 mL
6	onions, sliced	6
6	ears of corn on the cob	6
4 cups	vegetable stock	1 L
6 tbsp	heavy cream	90 mL
	freshly ground black pepper, to taste	
	freshly grated nutmeg, to taste	
	chopped fresh parsley, to garnish	

• Heat the oil in a large saucepan, add the onions and cook gently for 10–15 minutes, until softened, stirring occasionally.

• Meanwhile, cut away the corn from the cobs with a sharp knife, working lengthwise down each cob. Add the corn kernels to the onions with the stock and stir to mix. Bring to a boil, then reduce the heat.

• Cover and simmer for 10 minutes, until the corn is cooked and tender, stirring occasionally.

• Remove the pan from the heat and cool slightly, then purée in a food processor or blender until smooth. Return the soup to the rinsed-out pan, add the cream, pepper and nutmeg and reheat gently until hot, stirring occasionally.

• Ladle into warmed soup bowls and serve garnished with parsley.

Mixed Vegetable and Barley Soup

A satisfying soup enriched with sour cream. Serve with bread rolls or oatcakes.

Preparation time: 20 minutes, plus overnight soaking time · Cooking time 20–30 minutes · Serves: 6

½ cup	grains of rye, or wheat	125 mL
6 tbsp	pearl barley	90 mL
2½ cups	sauerkraut, thinly sliced	625 mL
2	green peppers, seeded and sliced	2
1	leek, thinly sliced	1
2	sticks of celery, thinly sliced	2
4	firm tomatoes, sliced	4
4	young carrots, thinly sliced	4
2 tsp	salt	10 mL
1 tsp	fennel seeds	5 mL
1 tsp	chopped fresh tarragon	5 mL
	freshly ground black pepper, to taste	
½ cup	milk	125 mL
½ cup	sour cream	125 mL
1 tbsp	chopped fresh dill	15 mL

• Place the rye and pearl barley in a bowl and cover with cold water. Leave to soak overnight.

• Place the prepared vegetables in a large saucepan with the soaked grains, soaking liquid and 2 cups (500 mL) water. Add the salt, fennel seeds, tarragon and pepper and stir to mix.

• Bring to a boil, then cover, reduce the heat and simmer for about 20–30 minutes, or until the vegetables and grains are cooked and tender, stirring occasionally. Stir in the milk, cream and dill, reheat gently, then ladle into warmed soup bowls to serve.

Gazpacho

Gazpacho

One of Spain's tastiest exports, this chilled soup makes an elegant starter.

Preparation time: 15 minutes · Serves: 4

1 lb	ripe tomatoes	450 g
1	small onion	1
1	small green pepper, seeded	1
1	clove of garlic, crushed	1
¼	medium cucumber, chopped	¼
1 tbsp	red wine vinegar	15 mL
1 tbsp	olive oil	15 mL
1	14-oz (398-mL) can of tomato juice	1
1–2 tbsp	lime juice	15–30 mL
	salt and freshly ground black pepper	
	croutons to garnish	

• Plunge the tomatoes into a bowl of boiling water, leave for 2 minutes, then plunge into a bowl of cold water. Remove and discard the skins and seeds. Set aside.

• Chop the onion and pepper and place in a food processor or blender with the tomatoes, garlic, cucumber, wine vinegar, oil and tomato juice.

• Purée until smooth and well mixed.

• Add the lime juice and seasoning to taste and blend to mix.

• Pour the soup into a glass dish, cover and chill until required.

• Ladle into soup bowls to serve and garnish each serving with a few croutons.

Serving suggestions: Serve with lightly buttered wholewheat bread.

Variations: Use plum tomatoes or yellow tomatoes in place of standard tomatoes. Use 1 small leek in place of the onion. Use cider vinegar in place of red wine vinegar.

COOK'S TIP

If the soup is too thick, add more tomato juice after adding the lime juice.

Cold Tomato Soup with Avocado Cream

A delicious fresh tomato soup — ideal for a summertime treat alfresco.

Preparation time: 20 minutes · Serves: 4

2 lb	ripe tomatoes	1 kg
4	shallots, finely chopped	4
⅓ cup	olive oil	80 mL
2½ tbsp	wine vinegar	40 mL
	salt and freshly ground black pepper	
2	small avocados	2
2	cloves of garlic, crushed	2
½ cup	milk	125 mL
2½ tbsp	lemon juice	40 mL
	sugar, to taste	
	fresh mint sprigs, to garnish	

• Chop the tomatoes, then purée in a food processor or blender until smooth. Press through a sieve and reserve the pulp, discarding the skin and seeds. Place the tomato pulp in a bowl.

• Stir the shallots, oil and wine vinegar into the tomato pulp and mix well. Season to taste with salt and pepper and set aside.

• For the avocado cream, peel and pit the avocados, then slice the flesh.

• Place the sliced avocados in a bowl, then mix with the garlic, milk, lemon juice, sugar and salt to taste.

• Blend the avocado mixture in a food processor or blender until smooth and well mixed.

• Serve the tomato soup in a soup bowl and spoon the avocado cream into the center of the soup.

• Serve, garnished with a sprig of fresh mint.

Serving suggestions: Serve with fresh crusty bread or toast.

Variations: Use plum tomatoes in place of standard tomatoes. Use sour cream in place of milk.

Chilled Tomato and Apricot Soup

An appetizing soup, full of refreshing flavor.

Preparation time: 20 minutes, plus cooling and chilling times · Cooking time: 10 minutes · Serves: 4

4 tbsp	butter	60 mL
4	shallots, thinly sliced	4
1	28-oz (796-mL) can of peeled tomatoes	1
	chopped fresh oregano or marjoram, to taste	
	salt and freshly ground black pepper	
	a large pinch of sugar	
1	28-oz (796-mL) can of apricots in juice	1
½ cup	dry white wine	125 mL
¾ cup	light (table) cream	175 mL
	fresh herb sprigs and croutons to garnish	

- Melt the butter in a pan, then add the shallots, tomatoes, oregano (or marjoram) and salt and pepper to taste.

- Cook gently for 10 minutes, stirring occasionally. Adjust the seasoning to make a piquant flavor, then add the sugar.

- Purée the mixture in a food processor or blender until smooth. Set aside to cool.

- Purée the apricots with the wine, ¼ cup (60 mL) water and cream in a food processor or blender until smooth.

- Pass the mixture through a sieve, discarding any pulp remaining in the sieve.

- Return the apricot mixture to the food processor or blender together with the cooled tomato mixture.

- Blend until thoroughly mixed, then pour into a bowl and chill before serving.

- Serve, garnished with fresh herb sprigs and croutons.

Serving suggestion: Serve with thin slices of wholewheat bread.

Variations: Use pears or peaches in place of apricots. Use unsweetened fruit juice such as apple or orange in place of wine.

COOK'S TIP

Instead of blending the tomato mixture and apricot purée together, chill separately, then swirl together in a serving bowl.

Split Pea Soup

A classic vegetarian soup that looks extra special with a swirl of yogurt on top.

Preparation time: 10 minutes · Cooking time: 40 minutes · Serves: 6

1 cup	split peas	250 mL
8 cups	vegetable stock, or water and a stock cube	2 L
2 tbsp	margarine	30 mL
1	large onion, chopped	1
3	sticks of celery, chopped	3
2	leeks, thinly sliced	2
2	medium potatoes, diced	2
1	medium carrot, finely chopped	1
	salt and freshly ground black pepper	
	leek slices, to garnish	

• Cook the split peas in the stock in a saucepan for 10–15 minutes, stirring occasionally.

• Meanwhile, melt the margarine in a separate pan, add the onion, celery and leeks. Cook for a few minutes, stirring occasionally.

• Add to the peas and stock together with the potatoes and carrot, and bring back to a boil.

• Reduce the heat, cover and simmer for 30 minutes, stirring occasionally.

• Remove from the heat and cool slightly, then purée in a food processor or blender until smooth.

• Return the blended mixture to the rinsed-out pan and reheat gently until piping hot, stirring occasionally.

• Season to taste with salt and pepper and ladle into warmed soup bowls to serve. Garnish with leek slices.

●

Serving suggestion: Serve with fresh bread or bread rolls.

Variations: Use green or brown lentils in place of split peas. Use sweet potatoes in place of standard potatoes. Use 1 parsnip in place of the carrot.

COOK'S TIPS
-
If the vegetables are chopped small enough, you can serve this as a chunky soup. If you do not have a food processor or blender, you can press the soup through a sieve, although it will not be quite as thick.

Fennel and Walnut Soup

A delicious and unusual combination of ingredients makes this soup ideal for serving as part of a special meal for four.

Preparation time: 15 minutes · Cooking time: 1 hour · Serves: 4

4 tsp	olive or sunflower oil	20 mL
1	small bulb fennel, chopped	1
1	head of celery, chopped	1
2	onions, chopped	2
¾ cup	shelled walnuts, crushed	175 mL
5 cups	vegetable stock, bean stock or water	1.25 L
¼ cup	Pernod	60 mL
⅔ cup	light cream	150 mL
	salt and freshly ground black pepper	
	fresh parsley sprigs, to garnish	

• Place the oil in a saucepan, add the fennel, celery and onion and cook over a low heat for 10 minutes, stirring occasionally.

• Add the walnuts and stock and bring to a boil. Cover and simmer for 45 minutes, stirring occasionally.

• Remove the pan from the heat, cool slightly, then purée the simmered ingredients in a blender or food processor, until smooth.

• Return to the rinsed-out pan, add the Pernod, cream, and salt and pepper; mix well.

• Reheat gently without boiling and serve garnished with fresh parsley sprigs.

Serving suggestion: Serve with thick slices of fresh crusty bread or bread rolls.

Variations: Other nuts such as cashew nuts or almonds can be used in place of walnuts. Use 2 leeks in place of the onions.

COOK'S TIP

Do not allow the soup to boil after adding the cream and Pernod, otherwise it may curdle.

French Onion Soup

This soup tastes best if cooked the day before serving and then reheated as required.

Preparation time: 10 minutes · Cooking time: 40 minutes · Serves: 4

3	medium onions	3
¼ cup	butter or vegetable margarine	60 mL
¼ cup	plain flour or soya flour	60 mL
5 cups	boiling vegetable stock (or water with 2 bouillon cubes)	1.25 L
	salt and freshly ground black pepper	
TOPPING		
4	slices of French bread, cut crosswise	4
½ cup	Cheddar cheese, grated	125 mL
¼ cup	Parmesan cheese, grated	60 mL

- Slice the onion very thinly into rings.

- Melt the butter or margarine in a pan, add the onion rings and fry over a medium heat until well browned.

- Add the flour and stir well until lightly browned.

- Gradually stir in the stock, then season with salt and pepper. Bring to a boil, stirring, then reduce the heat, cover and simmer for 30 minutes, stirring occasionally.

- Meanwhile, toast the bread on both sides.

- Mix the cheeses together, divide between the slices of toast and grill until melted and golden brown.

- Place the slices of toast and cheese in the bottom of individual soup dishes and spoon the soup over the top. Serve at once.

Serving suggestion: Serve with extra slices of French bread.

Variations: For a special occasion, add 2 tbsp (30 mL) brandy to the stock. Use 4 leeks or 12 shallots in place of the onion. Use Gruyère cheese in place of Cheddar.

COOK'S TIP

The onions must be very well browned to give a rich color and flavor to the soup.

99

Sweet Potato Soup

Warm up your winter nights with this heartening soup.

Preparation time: 10 minutes · Cooking time: 45–60 minutes · Serves: 4

2 tbsp	butter or margarine	30 mL
2	small onions, finely chopped	2
1 lb	sweet potatoes, peeled and diced	454 g
1¼ cups	carrots, diced	300 mL
4 tsp	chopped fresh coriander	20 mL
	rind and juice of 1 lemon	
3¼ cups	vegetable stock	800 mL
	freshly ground black pepper	
4	fresh coriander leaves, to garnish	4

• Melt the butter or margarine in a pan and cook the onion until transparent, stirring occasionally.

• Add the sweet potato and carrots and allow to 'sweat' over a very low heat for 10–15 minutes, stirring occasionally.

• Add the chopped coriander, lemon rind and juice, stock and pepper.

• Cover and simmer for 30 to 40 minutes, stirring occasionally.

• Cool slightly, then render in a food processor until almost smooth but leaving some texture to the soup.

• Return to the rinsed-out pan and reheat until piping hot, stirring occasionally.

• Garnish with a fresh coriander leaf and serve immediately.

Serving suggestion: Serve with wholegrain rolls.

Variations: Use fresh parsley or basil in place of coriander. Use standard potatoes in place of sweet potatoes. Use 3–4 small leeks in place of the onion. Use parsnips in place of carrots.

COOK'S TIP

Fresh coriander can be kept in a jug of water in a cool place. It can also be frozen for use when fresh is not available.

Snacks and
Appetizers

Watercress and Mushroom Paté

A quick-to-make and delightfully light paté made with low-fat cream cheese.

Preparation time: 10 minutes · Cooking time: 5 minutes · Serves: 4

3 tbsp	butter	45 mL
1	onion, finely chopped	1
1 cup	field mushrooms, finely chopped	250 mL
1	bunch of watercress, finely chopped	1
1 cup	low-fat cream cheese	250 mL
	a few drops of shoyu (Japanese soy sauce)	
½ tsp	caraway seeds	2.5 mL
	freshly ground black pepper	
	lime wedges, to garnish	

• Melt the butter in a saucepan over a low heat, add the onion and cook until soft but not colored, stirring occasionally.

• Increase the heat, add the field mushrooms and cook quickly for 2 minutes, stirring frequently.

• Add the chopped watercress and stir for about 30 seconds, until it becomes limp.

• Place the contents of the pan in a food processor or blender together with the cream cheese and shoyu. Blend until smooth and well mixed.

• Stir in the caraway seeds and pepper to taste.

• Place in individual ramekin dishes or one large serving dish, cover and chill for at least 2 hours, until firm, before serving. Garnish with lime wedges.

Serving suggestion: Serve with thin slices of lightly buttered brown bread or toast.

Variations: Use fresh wild mushrooms in place of field mushrooms. Use rocket leaves (arugula) in place of watercress. Use 4 shallots in place of the onion.

COOK'S TIP

It may be necessary to stir the contents of the food processor or blender several times, since the mixture should be fairly thick.

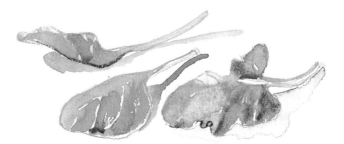

Tzatziki

A classic and refreshing starter or snack.

Preparation time: 10 minutes · Serves: 4–6

2	medium cucumbers	2
2¼ cups	plain yogurt	550 mL
1	clove of garlic, thinly sliced	1
2 tbsp	finely chopped fresh mint	30 mL
	olive oil, to taste	
	salt and freshly ground black pepper, to taste	
	fresh parsley sprigs, to garnish	

• Cut the cucumber in half lengthwise, then remove and discard the seeds and cut the flesh into small cubes. Place in a bowl.

• Add the yogurt and garlic and stir to mix well.

• Add the mint, olive oil and salt and pepper; mix well.

• Spoon into a dish and serve garnished with fresh parsley sprigs.

Serving suggestion: Serve with pita bread, black olives and raw, fresh vegetable crudités.

Variations: If available, use Greek yogurt or crème fraîche in place of plain yogurt. Use chopped fresh mixed herbs in place of mint.

COOK'S TIP

The cucumber can be coarsely grated rather than cut into cubes.

Hummus

A classic, flavorsome appetizer which also makes a perfect, satisfying snack.

Preparation time: 10 minutes, plus 1 hour standing time · Serves: 4

1 cup	cooked chickpeas (garbanzos), with the cooking liquid	250 mL
¼ cup	light tahini (sesame) paste	60 mL
	juice of 2 lemons	
6 tbsp	olive oil	90 mL
2–4	cloves of garlic, crushed	2–4
	salt, to taste	
	paprika and lemon wedges, to garnish	

• Place the cooked chickpeas in a blender with ⅔ cup (150 mL) of the reserved cooking liquid.

• Add the tahini, lemon juice, half the olive oil, garlic and salt.

• Blend until smooth, adding a little more cooking liquid if the mixture is too thick.

• Set aside for an hour or so to allow the flavors to develop.

• Serve in individual dishes with the remaining olive oil drizzled over the top. Serve sprinkled with paprika and garnished with lemon wedges.

Serving suggestions: Serve with warmed pita bread or vegetable crudités.

Variations: Use lime juice in place of lemon juice. Use flavored olive oil such as chili or herb oil in place of standard olive oil.

COOK'S TIP

Use canned, drained chickpeas instead of cooking your own. Use cold vegetable stock in place of the chickpea cooking liquid.

Hummus

Garlic Mushrooms

An established favorite, this recipe is very quick and easy to prepare.

Preparation time: 10 minutes · Cooking time: 10 minutes · Serves: 4

2 tbsp	butter or vegetable margarine	30 mL
2–3	cloves of garlic, crushed	2–3
	large pinch of chopped fresh thyme	
	large pinch of chopped fresh sage	
	large pinch of chopped fresh parsley	
¼ cup	white wine	50 mL
	salt and freshly ground black pepper	
4 cups	mushrooms, cleaned and quartered	1 L
8	slices of French bread, ½-in (1-cm) thick	8
2 tbsp	chopped fresh chives, to garnish	30 mL

• Melt the butter or margarine in a saucepan over a low heat.

• Add the garlic and cook for 1–2 minutes, or until soft and golden but not browned.

• Stir in the chopped herbs, wine, seasoning and mushrooms; mix well.

• Cover and simmer for about 5 minutes, or until the mushrooms are cooked but not soft, stirring occasionally.

• Warm through or lightly toast the bread on both sides.

• Place the bread on serving plates and pile equal amounts of the mushroom mixture onto each piece.

• Garnish with chopped chives and serving immediately.

Serving suggestions: Serve with sliced tomatoes or a small salad.

Variations: Use wild mushrooms in place of cultivated varieties. Use Italian ciabatta rolls in place of French bread.

COOK'S TIP

This recipe can be prepared well in advance and reheated just before serving.

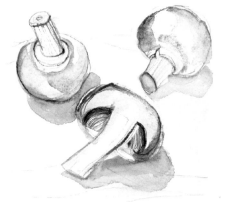

Fennel and Orange Croustade

Fragrant fennel and tangy orange combine perfectly to make an exciting topping for crisp, deep-fried bread.

Preparation time: 15 minutes · Cooking time: 5 minutes · Serves: 4

4	slices, 1-in (2.5-cm) thick, wholewheat bread	4
	oil, for deep frying	
2	fennel bulbs (reserve fronds for garnishing)	2
4	oranges	4
1½ tbsp	olive oil	20 mL
¼ tsp	salt	1 mL
	sprigs of fresh mint, to garnish	

COOK'S TIP

The salad can be made in advance and refrigerated until required but do not fill the bread case until just before serving.

• Trim and discard the crusts from the bread, then cut into 3-in (7.5-cm) squares.

• Hollow out the middle of the bread leaving an evenly shaped case.

• Heat the oil in a pan or deep-fat fryer and deep-fry the bread until golden brown. Carefully remove the bread from the hot oil.

• Drain the bread thoroughly on absorbent kitchen paper. Leave to cool.

• Trim the fennel, reserving the fronds, then thinly slice. Place in a bowl.

• Remove all the peel and pith from the oranges and cut into segments – do this over the bowl containing the fennel to catch the juice.

• Mix the orange segments with the fennel.

• Add the olive oil and salt and mix together thoroughly.

• Just before serving, pile the fennel and orange mixture into each bread case and garnish with a sprig of fresh mint and fennel fronds. Serve.

Serving suggestions: Serve with a mixed-leaf salad or crunchy coleslaw.

Variations: Use white or multigrain bread in place of wholewheat bread. Use 2 pink grapefruits in place of the orange. Use walnut or hazelnut oil in place of olive oil.

Vegetable Mini Pizzas

These flavorful vegetable snacks will make a welcome treat any time of day.

Preparation time: 20 minutes, plus kneading and rising time · Cooking time: 20 minutes · Serves: 4-6

PIZZA DOUGH

1 oz	fresh yeast (or 1 packet dry yeast)	40 g
2 cups	wholewheat flour	500 mL
	salt and freshly ground black pepper	
	fresh basil sprigs, to garnish	

TOPPING

4	tomatoes, sliced	4
	chopped fresh basil - or -	
3	small zucchinis, sliced	3
1½ tbsp	vegetable oil	20 mL
4	cloves garlic, crushed	4
	chopped fresh sage or basil	
¼ cup	grated hard cheese such as Old Cheddar or Parmesan	60 mL

• For the dough, crumble the yeast into a bowl and add ¼ cup (60 mL) lukewarm water. Stir the mixture to ensure there are no lumps. Leave to stand for 5 minutes.

• Sift the flour into a mixing bowl, make a well in the center of the flour and add a little salt and the yeast mixture.

• Add a further ¾ cup (175 mL) lukewarm water, mix in the flour, and then knead for about 5 minutes to form a smooth dough.

• Cover and leave to rise in a warm place until the dough has doubled in size.

• Roll out the dough until about ½-in (1-cm) thick. Cut out about 12 rounds with a pastry cutter.

• For the topping, cover the pizza bases with slices of tomato and chopped basil, then season with salt and pepper and sprinkle with cheese.

• If using zucchini topping instead of basil, cook the zucchini slices in hot oil in a pan with the garlic for 5 minutes. Season with salt to taste.

• Place the cooked zucchini slices on the pizza bases and sprinkle with the chopped herbs and cheese.

• Bake the mini pizzas in a preheated oven at 400°F/200°C for about 20 minutes, until cooked and golden brown. Serve hot or cold, garnished with fresh basil sprigs.

●

Serving suggestions: Serve with garlic or herb-flavored sour cream or plain yogurt.

Variations: Use white flour in place of wholewheat flour. Use 12–20 mushrooms, sliced, in place of the zucchini. Use fresh parsley or coriander in place of basil.

Crispy Lentil Strips

A substantial vegetarian appetizer, this dish is also good served on its own with a mint chutney.

Preparation time: 45 minutes, plus 4–5 hours soaking time · **Cooking time:** 25–30 minutes · **Serves:** 4–6

1 cup	split yellow lentils (chana daal)	250 mL
1 tbsp	coriander seeds	15 mL
1 tbsp	black peppercorns	15 mL
2 tsp	fresh ginger, peeled and chopped	10 mL
1 tbsp	fresh coriander, chopped	15 mL
2	green chilies, chopped	2
	salt, to taste	
1 tsp	red chili powder	5 mL
1 tsp	garam masala	5 mL
	vegetable oil, for frying	

COOK'S TIP

●

Take care when preparing fresh chilies. Wear rubber gloves or wash hands thoroughly after preparing chilies, since they contain volatile oils which can irritate and burn skin and eyes.

• Soak the lentils in cold water for 4–5 hours or in warm water for 30 minutes. Drain the lentils, then place them in a blender or food processor with the coriander seeds and peppercorns and grind to make a thick paste.

• Put the paste into a large bowl, add all the remaining ingredients, except the oil, mix thoroughly and set aside for 30 minutes.

• Heat the oil in a wok until it is smoking. With moist hands, shape the mixture into 4-in (10-cm) flat patties. Deep-fry the patties for 2–3 minutes on each side, then remove from the oil and drain on paper towels.

• Slice the patties into 3 or 4 strips. Reheat the oil until it is smoking, lower the heat to medium and deep-fry the patty strips until they are crisp and golden brown all over. Drain on absorbent kitchen paper, then serve immediately.

●

Serving suggestion: Serve with mint chutney.

Parsnip Fritters

These tasty fritters make a nice change for a light lunch or snack.

Preparation time: 10 minutes · **Cooking time:** 5–8 minutes per batch · **Serves:** 4

1 cup	plain unbleached flour	250 mL
2 tsp	baking powder	10 mL
1 tsp	salt	5 mL
½ tsp	freshly ground black pepper	2.5 mL
1	egg	1
⅔ cup	milk	150 mL
1 tbsp	melted butter	15 mL
3–4	cooked parsnips, finely diced	3–4
	oil or clarified butter, for frying	

• In a bowl, sift together the flour, baking powder, salt and pepper.

• Beat the egg in a small bowl and mix with the milk and melted butter.

• Stir the egg mixture into the dry ingredients.

• Stir in the cooked parsnips and mix well.

• Divide the mixture into 16 equal portions and shape into small fritters.

• Heat the oil or clarified butter in a frying pan. Fry the fritters in batches until browned on both sides, turning occasionally. Serve hot.

●

Serving suggestions: Serve with yogurt sauce or make them slightly larger and serve as a main course with salad.

Variations: Zucchinis, corn, onions or eggplant can be used in place of the parsnips.

Crispy Lentil Strips

Mixed Nut Balls

This versatile dish can be made in advance and refrigerated until required for cooking.

Preparation time: 20 minutes · Cooking time: 20–25 minutes · Serves: 8

⅔ cup	ground almonds	150 mL
⅔ cup	ground hazelnuts	150 mL
⅔ cup	pecans	150 mL
¾ cup	wholewheat breadcrumbs	175 mL
1 cup	Cheddar cheese, grated	250 mL
1	egg, beaten	1
4–5 tbsp	dry sherry - or - 2 tbsp (30 mL) milk and 3 tbsp (45 mL) dry sherry	60–75 mL
1	small onion, finely chopped	1
1 tbsp	grated fresh root ginger	15 mL
1 tbsp	chopped fresh parsley	15 mL
1	small red or green chili, seeded and finely chopped	1
1	medium red pepper, seeded and diced	1
1 tsp	sea salt	5 mL
1 tsp	freshly ground black pepper	5 mL
	lemon or lime slices, to garnish	

• Mix the almonds, hazelnuts and pecan nuts together with the breadcrumbs and cheese in a bowl. Set aside.

• In another bowl, mix the beaten egg with the sherry, onion, ginger, parsley, chili and red pepper.

• Combine with the nut mixture and add the salt and pepper. Mix well.

• If the mixture is too dry, add a little more sherry or milk.

• Form the mixture into small 1-in (2.5-cm) balls.

• Arrange the balls on a well greased baking tray and bake in a non-preheated oven at 350°F/180°C for about 20–25 minutes, until golden brown. Serve warm or cold, garnished with lemon or lime slices.

●

Serving suggestion: Serve on individual plates on a bed of chopped lettuce. Garnish with slices of lemon and serve along with your favorite sauce in a separate bowl.

Variations: Use ground walnuts in place of pecans. Use 1 shallot in place of the onion. Use 1 yellow or green pepper in place of the red pepper.

Mushroom Dumplings with Creamed Spinach

An unusual yet satisfying dish of mushroom-flavored dumplings served with spinach enriched with thickened cream.

Preparation time: 25 minutes · Cooking time: 30 minutes · Serves: 4–6

2 tbsp	butter	30 mL
2	onions, thinly sliced	2
1	8-oz (220-mL) can of mushrooms	1
1 tbsp	Cognac	15 mL
2	cloves of garlic, thinly sliced	2
6 tbsp	chopped fresh parsley	90 mL
1¼ cup	plain flour	300 mL
	about 1 cup (250 mL) milk	
½ cup	heavy cream	125 mL
2 tbsp	finely chopped shallots	30 mL
1 tbsp	green peppercorns	15 mL
6½ cups	fresh spinach leaves, torn and de-stemmed	1.6 L
1 tbsp	olive oil	15 mL
	salt and freshly ground black pepper	
1¼ cup	low-fat cottage cheese	300 mL
⅔ cup	sour cream	150 mL
	fresh herb sprigs, to garnish	

• Melt the butter in a pan, add the onion and cook until softened, stirring occasionally.

• Drain the mushrooms, finely chop, then add to the pan. Cook for about 5 minutes, stirring occasionally.

• Add the Cognac and 1 garlic clove. Increase the heat and cook until the juices in the pan are reduced, stirring frequently.

• Stir in the parsley, remove the pan from the heat and set aside to cool.

• In a bowl, mix the flour with the milk and cream, then stir in the mushroom mixture, shallots and peppercorns.

• Mold the mixture together and form into dumplings.

• Cook the dumplings in a saucepan of salted, boiling water for 10–15 minutes. Drain well and set aside to cool.

• Meanwhile, wash the spinach and cook in a saucepan with the olive oil, without adding any water, until wilted. Drain well and squeeze out any excess water. Chop the cooked spinach.

• Add the remaining garlic and season with salt and pepper to taste.

• Allow the spinach to cool, then mix with the cottage cheese and sour cream.

• Serve the dumplings with the creamed spinach alongside. Garnish with fresh herb sprigs.

●

Serving suggestions: Serve with a mixed leaf salad or crusty French bread.

Variations: Use broccoli florets in place of spinach leaves and boil for 5 minutes until tender. Mash well before adding the remaining ingredients. Use canned corn in place of mushrooms. Use chopped fresh basil in place of parsley.

Cheese and Pepper Bites

These colorful mini kebabs combine three different types of cheese with mixed peppers for an attractive and flavorful appetizer — ideal for a cocktail party or buffet.

Preparation time: 15 minutes · Cooking time: 15 minutes · Serves: 3–6

1	yellow pepper	1
1	red pepper	1
1	green pepper	1
1 tsp	olive oil	5 mL
	salt and freshly ground black pepper	
3 oz	sheep's cheese	85 g
3 oz	Gorgonzola	85 g
3 oz	Gouda or Cheddar cheese	85 g

• Brush the peppers all over with oil, then place on a baking tray.

• Bake in a preheated oven at 425°F/220°C for about 15 minutes, turning every 5 minutes, until blistered and brown.

• Remove the peppers from the oven, cover with a damp cloth and allow to cool slightly.

• Remove and discard the skin, seeds and cores from the peppers. Cut the flesh into strips, then season with salt and pepper.

• Cut each of the cheeses into equal sized pieces. Place the sheep's cheese on the yellow pepper strips, the Gorgonzola on the green pepper and the Gouda or Cheddar on the red pepper.

• Thread onto cocktail sticks or skewers and serve.

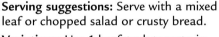

Serving suggestions: Serve with a mixed leaf or chopped salad or crusty bread.

Variations: Use 1 beefsteak tomato in place of the red pepper. There is no need to roast the tomato – simply remove the seeds and cut into strips. Use Blue, or Stilton in place of Gorgonzola.

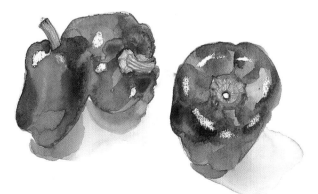

Savory Tomato

This light yet delicious dish is an ideal low-fat, low-calorie appetizer.

Preparation time: 10 minutes · Serves: 4

4	large beefsteak tomatoes	4
¼ cup	cottage cheese	60 mL
1 tsp	ground cumin	5 mL
2	green peppers, seeded and diced	2
	salt and freshly ground black pepper	
¼ cup	pumpkin seeds	60 mL
	sprigs of watercress, to serve	

- Slice off the top of each tomato.

- Remove and discard the seeds and leave the tomato upside down to drain.

- Rub the cottage cheese through a sieve to achieve a smooth consistency – add a little milk if necessary.

- Stir in the cumin, green pepper and salt and pepper to taste.

- Fill each tomato with the cheese mixture.

- Dry roast the pumpkin seeds in a frying pan until lightly browned. Sprinkle over the tomatoes. Chill until required.

- Serve on a bed of watercress sprigs.

Serving suggestions: Serve with thin slices of lightly buttered brown bread or crispbreads.

Variations: Use cream cheese in place of the cottage cheese. Use ground coriander in place of cumin. Use sunflower or sesame seeds in place of pumpkin seeds.

Watercress-Stuffed Potatoes

An unusual and delectable way of serving potatoes.

Preparation time: 20 minutes · **Cooking time:** 30 minutes (microwave) · **Serves:** 4

4	large baking potatoes	4
1 tbsp	vinegar	15 mL
2 tsp	salt	10 mL
4	eggs	4
1 tbsp	butter	15 mL
1 cup	mushrooms, sliced	250 mL
2	shallots, finely chopped	2
3 tbsp	margarine	45 mL
¼ cup	plain flour	60 mL
¼ tsp	dry mustard powder	1 mL
¼ tsp	cayenne pepper	1 mL
	salt and freshly ground black pepper	
1¼ cup	milk	300 mL
½ cup	Cheddar cheese, grated	125 mL
⅔ cup	milk	150 mL
1	bunch of watercress	1
	watercress sprigs and extra grated cheese, to garnish	

• Wash the potatoes and prick several times with a fork. Bake the potatoes in a microwave oven on HIGH for 10-12 minutes. Remove the potatoes from the oven and wrap completely in aluminium foil. Allow to stand for at least 5 minutes.

• Pour 5 cups (1.25 liters) hot water into a large, shallow dish. Add the vinegar and 2 tsp (10 mL) salt to the water. Heat on HIGH for 5 minutes, or until the water is boiling.

• Break the eggs, one at a time, into a cup and slide carefully into the vinegar water. Prick the yolks of each egg once with a sharp knife or skewer to prevent them from bursting. Cook on MEDIUM for 3 minutes. Fill a bowl with cold water and carefully remove each egg from the cooking liquid using a slotted spoon and stand in cold water until required.

• Melt the butter in a shallow bowl on HIGH for 30 seconds. Add the mushrooms and shallots to the butter and stir well. Cook on HIGH for 1 minute, then set aside.

• Melt the margarine in a bowl or jug on HIGH for 30 seconds. Stir the flour, mustard, cayenne and salt and pepper to taste into the melted margarine, mixing well with a wooden spoon to form a roux. Add 1¼ cup (300 mL) milk gradually to the flour mixture, cooking on HIGH for a total of 3 minutes, stirring well between each addition to make a smooth white sauce. Stir the grated cheese into the sauce and cook for 1 minute to melt. Set aside.

• Cut a slice off the top of each potato. Using a grapefruit knife or a spoon, carefully scoop the potato pulp out of each potato, taking care to leave a border inside each skin to form a firm shell. Reserve the potato pulp.

• Place equal amounts of the mushroom and shallot mixture into the base of each potato shell, and top with a well-drained egg. Spoon some cheese sauce over each egg.

• Heat the ⅔ cup (150 mL) remaining milk in a microwave-proof bowl in the microwave. Finely chop the watercress and mash the potato pulp. Beat together the watercress and mashed potato, then gradually whisk in the hot milk until the potato mixture is well blended and light.

• Pipe or spoon the mixture over the cheese sauce in the potato shells. Sprinkle the top of each potato with a little extra cheese and cook each potato on HIGH for 2–3 minutes to melt the cheese and heat through. Garnish with watercress sprigs and grated cheese and serve immediately.

●

Serving suggestion: Serve with homemade coleslaw or a chopped mixed salad.

Stuffed Zucchini

Creamed coconut and spices give this vegetable dish an exotic flavor.

Preparation time: 20 minutes · Cooking time: 30–45 minutes · Serves: 4

4	medium zucchinis	4
2 tbsp	olive oil	30 mL
2	small onions, very finely chopped	2
1	medium carrot, grated	1
½ tsp	paprika	2 mL
1 tsp	cumin seeds	5 mL
½ tsp	turmeric	2 mL
½ tsp	asafetida powder (optional)	2 mL
4 oz	creamed coconut, grated	100 g
	fresh herb sprigs, to garnish	

COOK'S TIP

Creamed coconut can be bought at delicatessens, healthfood shops and most supermarkets.

Asafetida powder is available from Indian food shops.

• Cut the zucchinis in half lengthwise.

• Using a teaspoon, remove the flesh leaving about a ¼-in (5-mm) shell.

• Finely chop the flesh and set aside.

• Heat the oil in a pan, add the onion and cook for a few minutes, stirring occasionally, until softened.

• Add the carrot, zucchini flesh and spices and cook, stirring frequently, for a further 5 minutes, until softened.

• Remove from the heat and stir in the creamed coconut.

• Pile the mixture into the zucchini shells, making sure that it covers the exposed part of the flesh.

• Place the zucchini halves in a greased ovenproof casserole dish and cook in a preheated oven at 375°F/190°C for 30–45 minutes, until the zucchini shells are soft.

• Serve immediately, garnished with fresh herb sprigs.

Serving suggestions: Serve the zucchini halves on their own as a snack, or with a parsley sauce and boiled new potatoes for a light lunch.

Variations: Use 4 small leeks or 4 shallots in place of onions. Use parsnips in place of carrot.

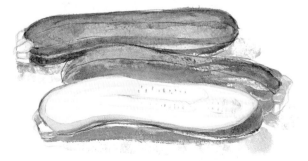

Pancakes Provençale

These light pancakes are filled with an inviting vegetable and cheese mixture.

Preparation time: 15 minutes · Cooking time: 1 hour · Serves: 4

½ cup	plain flour	125 mL
	large pinch of salt	
2	small eggs	2
⅔ cup	milk or water	150 mL
2 tbsp	olive oil	30 mL
2	small onions, finely chopped	2
2	cloves of garlic, crushed	2
2	small green peppers, seeded and diced	2
2	small red peppers, seeded and diced	2
2	small zucchinis, diced	2
2	tomatoes, skinned, seeded and chopped	2
1 tsp	chopped fresh basil	5 mL
2 tbsp	tomato paste	30 mL
¼ cup	Cheshire or Cheddar cheese, crumbled	60 mL
	salt and freshly ground black pepper	
	vegetable oil, for frying	
	fresh parsley sprigs, to garnish	

• Place the flour and salt in a bowl. Make a slight well in the center and break in the eggs.

• Using a wooden spoon, gradually incorporate the flour into the egg. Gradually add the milk or water and beat well to form a smooth batter. Set aside.

• Heat the olive oil in a pan over a medium heat, add the onion and garlic and cook for 2–3 minutes, until softened but not browned, stirring frequently.

• Add the peppers and zucchini and cook over a low heat for about 10 minutes, until softened, stirring frequently.

• Add the tomato, basil and tomato paste and cook for a further 5 minutes, stirring occasionally.

• Stir in the cheese, season to taste with salt and pepper and cook for a further 5 minutes, stirring occasionally. Set aside and keep warm.

• To cook the pancakes, heat a little vegetable oil in a small frying pan. Pour in just enough batter to thinly coat the base of the pan. Cook for 1–2 minutes, until golden brown.

• Turn over the pancake and cook the second side until golden brown. Remove from the pan and keep warm while you cook the remaining batter.

• Divide the vegetable mixture equally between each pancake and spread lightly with the back of a spoon.

• Roll up each filled pancake Swiss-roll style and place in an ovenproof serving dish.

• Place in a preheated oven at 350°F/180°C for 10 minutes, until hot.

• Serve, garnished with parsley sprigs.

Serving suggestion: Serve with a mixed leaf salad.

Variations: Omit the cheese from the filling and substitute halved pita breads for the pancakes to make a vegan variation.

Eggplant Slices in Yogurt

Eggplants can take a relatively long time to cook conventionally, and in the process can absorb a lot of cooking oil. Cooking them in the microwave with a delicious mixture of spices is the ideal choice.

Preparation time: 10 minutes, plus 30 minutes standing time · Cooking time: 2–4 minutes (microwave) · Serves: 4–6

2	large eggplants, cut into ¼-in (5-mm) thick rounds	2
	salt	
3 tbsp	olive oil	45 mL
1 tsp	chili powder	5 mL
¼ tsp	ground turmeric	1 mL
1 tsp	garam masala	5 mL
1	fresh green chili, seeded and thinly sliced	1
⅔ cup	plain yogurt	150 mL
	chopped fresh coriander leaves	
	paprika	

• Lightly score the eggplant rounds on both sides and sprinkle with salt. Place in a sieve over a bowl and leave to stand for 30 minutes, to drain the juices.

• Rinse the eggplant, drain and pat dry on absorbent kitchen paper.

• Heat the oil in a microwave-proof casserole dish in a microwave oven for 30 seconds on HIGH. Stir in the chili powder, turmeric, garam masala, chili and eggplant slices.

• Cover the casserole dish and cook in the microwave for 2–3 minutes on HIGH.

• Remove from microwave and pour the yogurt over top; set aside for 3–5 minutes.

• Sprinkle with the chopped coriander and paprika and serve hot or cold.

Serving suggestions: Serve with garlic and herb-flavored bread for a light meal, or serve as a side dish.

Variation: Use sour cream in place of ordinary plain yogurt for a richer and creamier dish.

Mixed Vegetables with Lemon Butter

Lightly cooked vegetables are served in a creamy, tangy sauce.

Preparation time: 15 minutes · Cooking time: 10 minutes · Serves: 4

2 lb	mixed vegetables, such as carrots, sugar-snap peas, kohlrabi and celery root	1 kg
½ cup	butter	125 mL
1½ tbsp	lemon juice	25 mL
	rind of 2 lemons	
	salt and freshly ground black pepper	
½–¾ cup	heavy cream	125–175 mL
¼ cup	chopped fresh chervil or chives	60 mL

• Peel or trim the vegetables, then cut into small pieces.

• Place the prepared vegetables in a shallow pan, add a little water and cover. Cook for about 10 minutes, until cooked and tender, stirring occasionally.

• Meanwhile, melt the butter in a pan, add the lemon juice and rind and salt and pepper to taste, then pour on the cream. Beat vigorously.

• Drain and serve the vegetables on a warm plate, sprinkle with the chopped herbs and pour the sauce over the top. Serve immediately.

Serving suggestions: Serve with garlic or herb-flavored bread or boiled rice.

Variations: Choose your own selection of mixed vegetables. Use lime or orange rind and juice in place of lemon. Use sour cream in place of cream.

Mixed Vegetable Curry

*A variety of seasonal vegetables are cooked together in an onion and tomato gravy with ground spices.
Whole green chilies are added towards the end of the cooking time to add flavor and fresh green color.*

Preparation time: 25–30 minutes · Cooking time: 30 minutes · Serves: 4–6

4–5 tbsp	vegetable oil	60–75 mL
1	large onion, finely chopped	1
1	½-in (1-cm) cube of fresh ginger, peeled and finely sliced	1
1 tsp	ground turmeric	5 mL
1 tsp	ground coriander	5 mL
1 tsp	ground cumin	5 mL
1 tsp	paprika	5 mL
4	small ripe tomatoes, skinned and chopped	4
1 cup	potatoes, peeled and diced	250 mL
¾ cup	green beans or dwarf beans, sliced	175 mL
1	medium carrot, scraped and sliced	1
¾ cup	shelled peas (fresh or frozen)	175 mL
2–4	whole green chilies	2–4
1 tsp	garam masala	5 mL
1 tsp	salt, or to taste	5 mL
1 tbsp	chopped fresh coriander leaves	15 mL

• Heat the oil in a large, heavy-based saucepan over a medium heat. Add the onion and fry for 6–7 minutes, until lightly browned, stirring frequently. Add the ginger and fry for 30 seconds, stirring.

• Reduce the heat to low and add the turmeric, coriander, cumin and paprika. Stir to mix well.

• Add half the tomatoes and cook for 2 minutes, stirring continuously.

• Add all the vegetables and 2 cups (500 mL) warm water to the pan and stir well. Bring to a boil, cover and simmer for 15–20 minutes, until the vegetables are tender.

• Add the remaining tomatoes and green chilies and stir to mix. Cover and simmer for a further 5–6 minutes.

• Add the garam masala, salt and half the chopped coriander, stir well, then remove the pan from the heat.

• Transfer the curry to a warmed serving dish and sprinkle with the remaining chopped coriander. Serve immediately.

COOK'S TIP

This dish is suitable for freezing, but omit the potatoes. Add preboiled diced potatoes during reheating.

Serving suggestion: Serve with naan bread or warmed wholewheat pita bread.

Variations: Use your own selection of fresh vegetables in season. Use a small can of tomatoes in place of the fresh tomatoes.

Cauliflower and Cabbage in Walnut Cheese Sauce

This is a delicious, up-market version of the humble cauliflower with cheese.

Preparation time: 15 minutes · Cooking time: 19 minutes (microwave on HIGH) · Serves: 4

1	cauliflower	1
1	small green cabbage	1
4 tbsp	butter	60 mL
½ cup	wholewheat flour	125 mL
2¼ cups	milk	600 mL
1 cup	Cheddar cheese, grated	250 mL
¾ cup	shelled walnuts, chopped	175 mL
	grated nutmeg, to garnish	

• Break the cauliflower into small florets. Coarsely shred the cabbage.

• Place the cauliflower and cabbage in a large microwave-proof bowl with ½ cup (125 mL) water. Cover the bowl with plastic wrap and pierce several times with the tip of a sharp knife.

• Cook the vegetables in a microwave oven on HIGH for 10 minutes, or until they are cooked but still slightly crunchy.

• Place the butter and flour in a microwave-proof bowl and mix together with a fork. Blend in the milk and cook on HIGH for 2 minutes.

• Stir the sauce well and cook on HIGH for a further 2 minutes.

• Add the cheese and walnuts to the sauce and mix well to blend thoroughly. Cook on HIGH for 2 minutes to melt the cheese.

• Drain the vegetables thoroughly and transfer to a serving dish. Pour over the sauce and cook on HIGH for a few minutes before serving. Serve immediately, sprinkled with nutmeg.

Serving suggestion: Serve with a tomato and onion salad.

Variations: Use broccoli florets in place of cauliflower. Use red cabbage in place of green cabbage. Use Blue cheese in place of Cheddar.

COOK'S TIP

Use a whisk when preparing the sauce mixture to prevent any lumps from forming.

Ratatouille

A flavorful version of this famous and ever-appealing mixed Mediterranean vegetable stew. Choose top quality, fresh ingredients for the best results.

Preparation time: 15 minutes · Cooking time: 50 minutes · Serves: 4

2	small eggplants		2
	salt		
3 tbsp	olive oil		45 mL
2	onions, thinly sliced		2
4	cloves of garlic, crushed		4
2	beefsteak tomatoes, skinned		2
2	small zucchinis, sliced		2
2	small red peppers, seeded and sliced		2
2 cups	mushrooms, sliced		500 mL
2 tsp	tomato paste		10 mL
2	bay leaves		2
	large pinch of dried thyme		
	large pinch of dried rosemary		
	large pinch of dried marjoram		
	freshly ground black pepper		
	fresh herb sprigs, to garnish		

• Slice the eggplants, place in a colander and sprinkle with salt. Set aside for 10 minutes, then rinse, drain and pat dry with absorbent kitchen paper. Set aside.

• Heat the oil in a saucepan. Add all the vegetables, tomato paste, bay leaves, dried herbs and pepper to the pan and stir well to mix.

• Cover the pan and cook over a low heat for about 50 minutes, or until the vegetables are cooked and tender, stirring occasionally. Remove and discard the bay leaves.

• Serve, garnished with fresh herb sprigs.

Serving suggestions: Serve with small oven-baked potatoes or hunks of fresh crusty bread.

Variations: Use 4 leeks in place of the onions. Use 2 small yellow or green peppers in place of the red peppers. Use 4–6 plum tomatoes in place of the beefsteak tomato.

COOK'S TIP

Use ratatouille as a filling for stuffed peppers or hollowed out eggplants, or use as a filling for crêpes or a topping for baked potatoes.

Indonesian-Style Okra

An interesting vegetable dish of okra, tomatoes and onions flavored with fresh parsley.

Preparation time: 15 minutes · **Cooking time:** 25 minutes · **Serves:** 4–6

2¼ lb	okra	1 kg
3 tbsp	spiced vinegar	45 mL
2 tbsp	olive oil	30 mL
2	onions, thinly sliced	2
10	tomatoes, skinned and chopped	10
	salt and freshly ground black pepper	
3 tbsp	chopped fresh parsley	45 mL
2 cups	vegetable stock	500 mL
	fresh parsley sprigs, to garnish	

• Top and tail the okra, then blanch in a saucepan of boiling water for about 3 minutes.

• Place the okra in a colander, sprinkle with vinegar, then drain well and set aside.

• Heat the oil in a frying pan, add the okra and onions and cook until the okra change color and the onion softens, stirring continuously.

• Add the tomatoes, salt and pepper and parsley to the pan, then add the stock.

• Bring to a boil, cover, then reduce the heat and simmer for 10 to 15 minutes, until the vegetables are cooked and tender, stirring occasionally.

• Serve hot, garnished with fresh parsley sprigs.

Serving suggestions: Serve with warm Italian ciabatta rolls or oven-baked potatoes.

Variations: Use sesame oil in place of olive oil. Use fresh basil in place of parsley.

Garlic Baby New Potatoes

These delectable pan-fried potatoes flavored with garlic, fresh thyme and green onions make a great snack or side dish.

Preparation time: 10 minutes · Cooking time: 20–25 minutes · Serves: 2–4

1¼ lb	baby new potatoes	500 g
1	bunch of green onions	1
2 tbsp	olive oil	30 mL
10	small fresh cloves of garlic	10
	salt and freshly ground black pepper	
1 tbsp	finely chopped fresh thyme	15 mL

• Scrub the potatoes with a brush. Remove and discard the roots and darker green foliage from the green onions and cut in half lengthwise.

• Heat the oil in a pan, add the potatoes and cook until evenly lightly browned all over, stirring frequently.

• Add the green onions and garlic and cook for about 5 minutes, stirring occasionally.

• Season with salt and pepper and sprinkle with the thyme.

• Add a little water and cook for a further 10–15 minutes, until the potatoes are cooked and tender, stirring occasionally. Serve hot.

Serving suggestion: Serve as an accompaniment to grilled or roast mixed vegetables, such as eggplants, peppers and zucchinis.

Variations: Use sesame oil in place of olive oil. Use fresh marjoram, oregano or chives in place of thyme.

COOK'S TIP

Do not let the garlic brown too much, or it will taste bitter.

Curried Potatoes

These spicy potatoes make a satisfying snack or side dish.

Preparation time: 10 minutes · Cooking time: 25 minutes · Serves: 4

2¼ lb	potatoes	1 kg
	salt	
¼ cup	vegetable oil	60 mL
4	onions, thinly sliced	4
1	1½-inch (3.5-cm) piece of fresh ginger, finely chopped	1
4	cloves of garlic, crushed	4
2 tsp	curry powder	10 mL
¼–½ cup	sesame seeds	60–120 mL

• Peel the potatoes and cut into cubes.

• Season the potato cubes with salt, then heat the oil in a pan and cook the potatoes for 10 minutes, turning frequently to cook evenly.

• Add the onion, ginger, garlic and curry powder to the potatoes.

• Add about ¾ cup (175 mL) water to the pan and stir to mix. Cover and cook for 10–12 minutes, stirring occasionally, until the potatoes are cooked and tender.

• Taste and adjust the seasoning and serve immediately, sprinkled with sesame seeds.

●

Serving suggestion: Serve with a shredded vegetable salad.

Variations: Use 4 leeks in place of the onions. Use sweet potatoes in place of standard potatoes. Use chili powder in place of curry powder.

COOK'S TIP

●

Curry paste can be used in place of curry powder.

Main Dishes

Chickpea Flour Dumplings in a Yogurt Curry

A hot, satisfying vegetarian dish, ideal when served with boiled rice.

Preparation: 30 minutes · Cooking: 1 hour · Serves: 4

1½ cup	plain yogurt	375 mL
	salt, to taste	
1 tsp	red chili powder	5 mL
1 tsp	ground turmeric	5 mL
1¼ cup	chickpea (or gram) flour	300 mL
	pinch of bicarbonate of soda	
½ tsp	carom seeds	2 mL
5	green chilies, chopped	5
¼ cup	peanut oil, plus extra for frying	60 mL
¾ cup	potatoes, cut into rounds	175 mL
¾ cup	onions, cut into ¼-in (5-mm) thick rounds	175 mL
½ tsp	cumin seeds	2 mL
¼ tsp	mustard seeds	1 mL
¼ tsp	fenugreek seeds	1 mL
4	whole red chilies	4

• Whisk the yogurt, salt, red chili powder, turmeric and half the chickpea flour together in a bowl. Set aside.

• Sift the remaining chickpea flour and bicarbonate of soda together, add the carom seeds and enough water to make a thick batter. Beat well. Stir in the green chilies.

• Heat enough oil in a wok to deep-fry. Drop large spoonfuls of the batter into the oil to form 1½-in (4-cm) puffy dumplings. Fry until golden brown on all sides. Remove from the pan, set aside and keep warm.

• Heat 3 tbsp (45 mL) oil in a saucepan and add the yogurt mixture and 2¾ cups (700 mL) water. Bring to a boil, reduce the heat and simmer for 8–10 minutes, stirring constantly to prevent the yogurt curdling.

• Add the potatoes and onions and cook until the potatoes are tender. Add the dumplings, simmer for 35 minutes, stirring occasionally, then remove from the heat and transfer to a serving bowl.

• Heat the remaining 1 tbsp (15 mL) oil in a small pan. Add the cumin, mustard and fenugreek seeds and cook until they crackle. Add the whole red chilies, remove from the heat and pour over the hot curry. Serve immediately.

Serving suggestion: Serve hot, garnished with chopped fresh coriander and accompanied by boiled white or brown rice.

Mixed Grain Patties

These tempting, crispy snacks are fragrantly flavored with fennel and served sprinkled with grated cheese.

Preparation time: 15 minutes · Cooking time: 15 minutes · Serves: 2–4

1½ cup	quark, or low-fat cottage cheese	375 mL
1¼ cup	plain wholewheat flour	300 mL
1 tsp	salt	5 mL
	freshly ground black pepper, to taste	
	grated nutmeg, to taste	
1	bunch of green onions, finely sliced	1
1	bulb of fennel, sliced	1
1¼ cup	wheat grains, cooked	300 mL
1¼ cup	pearl barley, cooked	300 mL
⅓ cup	sunflower seeds	75 mL
3½ tbsp	vegetable margarine	50 mL
¾ cup	Emmenthal cheese, grated	175 mL

• Drain the quark thoroughly. In a bowl, mix the quark with the flour, salt, pepper, nutmeg and prepared vegetables.

• Mix the wheat grains and pearl barley with the sunflower seeds and add to the quark mixture. Mix well.

• Heat the margarine in a frying pan, then add the grain mixture. Spread out over the base of the pan and fry for about 5 minutes, until it has formed a crust, then turn and fry the other side until crispy.

• Break apart with 2 forks and fry the pieces for a further 2 minutes. Sprinkle with the grated cheese to serve.

Serving suggestions: Serve with a mixed dark leaf salad or a mixed pepper, tomato and onion salad.

Variations: Use pumpkin or sesame seeds in place of sunflower seeds. Use white flour in place of wholewheat flour. Use Cheddar cheese in place of Emmenthal.

Nutty Potato Cakes

This is the perfect way to use up leftover potatoes to create a tasty snack.

Preparation time: 10 minutes · Cooking time: 25 minutes · Serves: 4

3	medium potatoes	3
2 tbsp	butter	10 mL
	a little milk	
¾ cup	mixed nuts, finely ground	175 mL
¼ cup	sunflower seeds, finely ground	60 mL
2 tbsp	green onion, finely chopped	30 mL
	freshly ground black pepper	
	wholewheat flour, for coating	
	vegetable oil, for frying	

• Peel the potatoes and cut into pieces. Cook in a pan of boiling water until just soft.

• Drain and mash the potatoes with butter and milk to a creamy consistency.

• Add the nuts, seeds, green onion and pepper to taste, mixing well.

• If necessary, add a little more milk at this stage to give a soft texture which holds together.

• Form the mixture into 8 round cakes. Coat with flour and fry quickly in a frying pan in a little oil until golden brown on both sides.

• Drain on absorbent paper towel and serve hot.

Serving suggestion: Serve with a green salad and sliced tomatoes in an oil and fresh basil dressing.

Variations: Dry-roast the sunflower seeds until golden brown before grinding, if you like. Use sweet potatoes in place of standard potatoes.

Chickpea Burgers

These burgers are delicious served hot or cold, and make great picnic food.

Preparation time: 15 minutes, plus 1 hour chiling time · **Cooking time:** 10–15 minutes · **Serves:** 4

2½ cups	(or 2 14-oz (398-mL) cans) cooked chickpeas, drained	625 mL
2	small onions, finely chopped	2
2	cloves of garlic, crushed	2
2	medium potatoes, cooked and mashed	2
2 tbsp	shoyu (Japanese soy sauce)	30 mL
2 tsp	lemon juice	10 mL
	freshly ground black pepper	
	plain wholewheat flour, for coating	
	vegetable oil, for frying	
	fresh parsley sprigs, to garnish	

• Place the chickpeas in a large bowl and mash well.

• Add the onion, garlic, mashed potatoes, shoyu, lemon juice and pepper. Mix together thoroughly.

• With floured hands, shape heaped tablespoonfuls of the mixture into small burgers.

• Coat each burger with flour, place on a plate and refrigerate for 1 hour.

• Heat a little oil in a frying pan and gently fry the burgers on each side until golden brown. Serve hot or cold, garnished with fresh parsley sprigs.

Serving suggestion: Serve with a hot, spicy tomato sauce or relish.

Variations: Use cooked or canned red kidney beans in place of chickpeas. Use sweet potatoes in place of standard potatoes. Use 2 small leeks in place of the onions.

COOK'S TIP

Cook the burgers, allow to cool, then wrap and freeze for up to 2 months.

Sweet-and-Sour Nuggets

These crunchy, Asian-style bites are sure to please.

Preparation time: 30 minutes, plus chilling time · Cooking time: 15 minutes · Serves: 4

2 tbsp	butter or margarine	30 mL
1	shallot, peeled and finely chopped	1
¼ cup	plain flour	60 mL
⅔ cup	milk	150 mL
½ cup	ground almonds	125 mL
½ cup	water chestnuts, finely chopped	125 mL
1 tsp	chopped fresh parsley	5 mL
1 tsp	ground ginger	5 mL
1	egg, beaten	1
	salt and freshly ground black pepper	
	dry breadcrumbs, for coating	
	sesame seeds, for coating	
¼ cup	peanut oil, for frying	60 mL
¼ cup	soft brown sugar	60 mL
¼ cup	vinegar	60 mL
2 tbsp	ketchup	30 mL
2 tbsp	soy sauce	30 mL
1	8-oz (225-g) can of pineapple chunks	1
3 tbsp	cornstarch	45 mL
1	green pepper, seeded and sliced	1
2	green onions, trimmed and cut into thin diagonal slices	2
1	small can of bamboo shoots, drained	1
½ lb	fresh bean sprouts	225 g

• Heat the butter in a large wok or frying pan. Add the shallot and stir well to coat evenly. Cook for 1 minute or until softened. Stir the flour into the shallot mixture, blending it well with a wooden spoon to form a paste. Gradually add the milk, beating well and cooking for 30 seconds between additions, until the sauce is thick and smooth.

• Stir in the almonds, water chestnuts, parsley, ginger, half the beaten egg and some seasoning, mixing well to form a thick paste.

• Place the almond paste in a dish and chill in the refrigerator until firm. Divide the chilled mixture into 16 evenly sized balls.

• Place the breadcrumbs and the sesame seeds into a dish and mix together thoroughly. Brush each almond nugget with the remaining beaten egg, then coat in the breadcrumbs and sesame seed mixture.

• Heat the peanut oil in a frying pan over high heat. Add the coated nuggets and fry for 4 to 5 minutes, or until browned all over. Drain the nuggets on paper towels and keep warm while preparing the sauce.

• Mix together the sugar, vinegar, ketchup and soy sauce in a deep-sided bowl or jug. Drain the juice from the pineapple and stir into the vinegar mixture. Reserve the pineapple chunks. Blend the cornstarch into the sauce liquid, whisking until smooth. Cook, stirring, over high heat for 2 to 3 minutes. Reduce heat to medium.

• Add the pepper, onions and bamboo shoots to the sauce. Chop the pineapple chunks into small pieces and stir into the sauce, mixing all the ingredients together thoroughly. Cook for 3 to 4 minutes, or until heated through.

• Arrange the bean sprouts on a serving dish and place the warm nuggets on top. Pour a little of the sauce over the nuggets and serve any remaining sauce separately.

●

Serving suggestion: Serve accompanied with a crisp, green salad, and boiled or Asian-style egg-fried rice.

Mushrooms and Tofu in Garlic Butter

This inviting dish – ideal for a light lunch or supper – is quick and easy to make.

Preparation time: 10 minutes · Cooking time: 10–12 minutes · Serves: 4

½ cup	butter	125 mL
4	small cloves of garlic, crushed	4
1	1-in (2.5-cm) piece of fresh root ginger, grated	1
3 cups	button mushrooms	750 mL
8 oz	smoked tofu (or see *Cook's Tip* below), cubed	220 g
2½ tbsp	chopped fresh parsley	40 mL

COOK'S TIP

Ready-prepared fresh root ginger is available in jars, to save a little time.

• Melt the butter in a frying pan. Add the garlic and ginger and fry gently for 2 minutes, stirring occasionally.

• Add the mushrooms and cook gently for 4–5 minutes, until the mushrooms are softened, stirring occasionally.

• Add the smoked tofu and cook gently until hot, stirring occasionally.

• Place on a warm plate, sprinkle with chopped parsley and serve at once.

Serving suggestions: Serve with crusty French bread or a crusty wholewheat rolls.

Variations: Use asparagus tips in place of mushrooms. Use regular tofu for a change. Use fresh basil or coriander in place of parsley.

Smoked Tofu Salad

A tasty main course salad – ideal served with fresh bread.

Preparation time: 15 minutes · Serves: 4

2 cups	broccoli florets	500 mL
1½ cups	mushrooms	375 mL
⅓ cup	pineapple chunks	75 mL
¼ cup	canned corn, drained	60 mL
¼ cup	French (oil and vinegar) dressing	60 mL
8 oz	smoked tofu (or see *Cook's Tip* below), cut into cubes	220 g

COOK'S TIP

If smoked tofu is unavailable, use regular tofu and marinate for a few hours in equal parts of shoyu (Japanese soy sauce) and olive oil with a little crushed garlic and fresh grated ginger.

• Cover the broccoli florets with boiling water in a bowl and leave to stand for 5 minutes. Drain and allow to cool.

• Thinly slice the mushrooms.

• Cut the pineapple into small pieces.

• Place the broccoli, mushrooms, pineapple and corn in a bowl together with the French dressing. Mix carefully.

• Place the salad on a serving dish and place the smoked tofu on top. Serve at once.

Serving suggestions: Serve with warmed Italian ciabatta rolls or pita bread.

Variations: Omit the tofu and serve as a side salad with savory vegetable flans. Use cauliflower florets in place of broccoli. Use mango in place of pineapple. Use canned chickpeas or kidney beans, rinsed and drained, in place of corn.

Mushrooms and Tofu in Garlic Butter

Bulgur Risotto

A colorful risotto combining mixed peppers, corn, peas, and peanuts with soft bulgur wheat.

Preparation time: 15 minutes · Cooking time: 20 minutes · Serves: 4

1 cup	bulgur wheat	250 mL
1 tbsp	butter	15 mL
2	small onions, finely chopped	2
2	sticks of celery, finely chopped	2
2	cloves of garlic, crushed	2
1	small red pepper, diced	1
1	small green pepper, diced	1
½ tsp	dried mixed herbs	2 mL
½ cup	peanuts, chopped	125 mL
1 tsp	vegetable extract, dissolved in 1 cup (250 mL) boiling water	5 mL
2 tsp	shoyu sauce (Japanese soy sauce)	10 mL
¾ cup	corn kernels	175 mL
¾ cup	frozen peas	175 mL
	salt and freshly ground black pepper	
	juice of 1 lemon	

• Place the bulgur wheat in a bowl and cover with boiling water. Stir to mix.

• Leave for about 10 minutes, or until the water is absorbed and the wheat is swollen.

• Meanwhile, melt the butter in a saucepan, add the onion, celery and garlic and cook for a few minutes, stirring frequently, until softened but not browned.

• Add the peppers, herbs, peanuts and vegetable extract and water.

• Bring to a boil, reduce the heat and simmer over a low heat for about 8 minutes, stirring occasionally.

• Add the bulgur wheat, shoyu, corn, peas and salt and pepper to taste and mix together well. Continue cooking for a further 5 minutes, stirring occasionally.

• Mix in the lemon juice and transfer to a warmed serving dish. Serve immediately.

Serving suggestion: Serve with a crisp green salad and toasted pita breads.

Variations: Use couscous in place of bulgur wheat. Use hazelnuts or almonds in place of peanuts. Use frozen baby broad beans or canned, drained chickpeas or red kidney beans in place of peas.

COOK'S TIP

If the risotto is too dry, add a little more water or stock. Sprinkle with finely grated fresh Parmesan cheese before serving.

Spanish Barley

Paprika gives this colorful and tasty dish — cooked in the microwave for convenience — its distinctive taste. Whether served hot or cold, it is equally good.

Preparation time: 15 minutes · Cooking time: 26 minutes (microwave on HIGH) · Serves: 4

2½ cups	pearl barley	625 mL
2½ cups	vegetable stock or water	625 mL
2	Spanish onions, peeled and chopped	2
2	cloves of garlic, crushed	2
2	small green pepper, seeded and chopped	2
1½ tbsp	olive or vegetable oil	20 mL
1 tsp	paprika	5 mL
1 tsp	salt	5 mL
3 cups	canned tomatoes, roughly chopped	750 mL
	tomato slices and chopped fresh parsley, to garnish	

• Place the pearl barley in a microwave-proof bowl with the stock or water. Cook in a microwave oven on HIGH for 20 minutes.

• Drain any excess water from the pearl barley and set aside.

• Place the onion, garlic and green pepper in a microwave-proof bowl with the oil. Stir to mix, then cook on HIGH for 2 minutes. Set aside.

• Place the drained pearl barley in a large microwave-proof bowl. Stir the paprika, salt and tomatoes into the cooked pearl barley. Stir well to combine the ingredients thoroughly.

• Add the vegetables to the tomato and pearl barley mixture and stir well.

• Cover the bowl with plastic wrap and pierce several times with the tip of a sharp knife.

• Cook on HIGH for 4 minutes, then allow the dish to stand for 5 minutes before serving, to give the flavor of the paprika time to develop. Serve, garnished with tomato slices and chopped parsley.

Serving suggestion: Serve with a tomato and basil salad and French bread.

Variations: Add ¾ cup (175 mL) pitted and sliced black olives and ½ cup (125 mL) cubed Feta cheese for a tangy alternative. Use 1 red or yellow pepper in place of the green pepper

COOK'S TIP

This recipe freezes successfully for up to 3 months. The flavor of the paprika will be enhanced during this time.

Vegetarian Paella

This easy-to-prepare dish is full of color and interesting texture.

Preparation time: 15 minutes · **Cooking time:** 1 hour · **Serves:** 4–6

¼ cup	olive oil	60 mL
1	large onion, chopped	1
2	cloves of garlic, crushed	2
½ tsp	paprika	2.5 mL
1½ cups	long-grain brown rice	375 mL
3½ cups	vegetable stock	875 mL
¾ cup	dry white wine	175 mL
1	14-oz (398-mL) can of tomatoes, plus juice, chopped	1
1 tbsp	tomato paste	15 mL
½ tsp	dried tarragon	2.5 mL
1 tsp	dried basil	5 mL
1 tsp	dried oregano	5 mL
1	red pepper, seeded and roughly chopped	1
1	green pepper, seeded and roughly chopped	1
3	sticks of celery, finely chopped	3
3 cups	mushrooms, sliced	750 mL
½ cup	snow peas, topped, tailed and cut in half	125 mL
1 cup	frozen peas	250 mL
½ cup	cashew nut pieces	125 mL
	salt and freshly ground black pepper	
	chopped fresh parsley, lemon wedges and olives, to garnish	

• Heat the oil in a saucepan or paella pan and fry the onion and garlic until soft.

• Add the paprika and rice and continue to cook for 4–5 minutes, until the rice is transparent, stirring occasionally.

• Add the stock, wine, tomatoes, tomato paste and herbs and simmer for 10–15 minutes, stirring occasionally.

• Add the peppers, celery, mushrooms and snow peas and continue to cook for a further 30 minutes, until the rice is cooked, stirring occasionally. Add a little extra stock, if necessary.

• Add the peas, cashew nuts and seasoning to taste.

• Cook until the peas are cooked, then place on a large heated serving dish.

• Sprinkle the parsley over the top and garnish with lemon wedges and olives. Serve.

●

Serving suggestion: Serve with crusty French bread and a mixed dark leaf salad.

Variations: Use a mixture of brown and wild rice for a change. Use unsweetened apple juice in place of white wine. Use fresh wild mushrooms in place of cultivated mushrooms.

COOK'S TIP

●

To prepare in advance, undercook slightly, add a little more stock or water and reheat. Do not add the peas until just before serving, otherwise they will lose their color.

Red Lentils with Vegetables

This tasty combination of red lentils and vegetables makes a warming and filling main course dish.

Preparation time: 15 minutes, plus overnight soaking · Cooking time: 45–60 minutes · Serves: 4

1¾ cups	red lentils	425 mL
2 tbsp	olive oil	30 mL
2	cloves of garlic, crushed	2
1	onion, cut into small chunks	1
1	carrot, cut into small chunks	1
1	leek, cut into small chunks	1
1	stick of celery, cut into small chunks	1
2–3 tbsp	tomato paste	30–45 mL
2¼ cups	vegetable stock	550 mL
2 tbsp	white wine vinegar	30 mL
1	sprig of fresh thyme	1
	salt and freshly ground black pepper	
	pinch of cayenne pepper	
2 tbsp	honey	30 mL
1	bunch of fresh chives	1
	slices of leek, to garnish	

• Wash the lentils thoroughly under cold running water, then drain well. Place the lentils in a bowl, cover with water and leave to soak overnight.

• Heat the oil in a pan, add the garlic and cook until softened. Add the prepared vegetables and cook briefly, stirring.

• Stir in the tomato paste and stock, then bring to the boil.

• Drain the lentils thoroughly, add to the pan and stir well. Cover and simmer for 30–40 minutes, until the vegetables and lentils are almost cooked and tender, stirring occasionally.

• Stir in the wine vinegar and thyme. Season with salt and pepper and cayenne, then stir in the honey.

• Continue cooking over a moderate heat for a further 10–15 minutes, stirring occasionally.

• Meanwhile, finely chop the chives, leaving a few leaves whole for garnishing.

• Once the dish is cooked, adjust the seasoning and serve sprinkled with chopped chives.

• Garnish with slices of leek and whole chive leaves.

Serving suggestions: Serve with French bread and a green salad or cooked fresh vegetables such as broccoli and carrots.

Variations: Use green or brown lentils in place of red lentils. Use chili powder in place of cayenne pepper. Use fresh parsley or basil in place of chives.

Savory Bean Pot

A hearty and spicy dish for a satisfying meal the family will love.

Preparation time: 20 minutes · Cooking time: 30 minutes · Serves: 4

2½ tbsp	vegetable oil	40 mL
2	vegetable flavored bouillon cubes, crumbled	2
4	small onions, chopped	4
2	apples, peeled and grated	2
4	small carrots, grated	4
¼ cup	tomato paste	60 mL
2 tbsp	white wine vinegar	30 mL
2 tsp	dried mustard	10 mL
½ tsp	dried oregano	2 mL
½ tsp	ground cumin	2 mL
2 tsp	brown sugar	10 mL
	salt and freshly ground black pepper	
3 cups	cooked (or canned) red kidney beans	750 mL
	a little sour cream	

- Heat the oil in a non-stick pan. Add the crumbled bouillon cube, onion, apple and carrot.

- Cook gently for 5 minutes, stirring continuously.

- In a bowl, mix the tomato paste with 1¼ cup (300 mL) water and add to the pan together with all the other ingredients, except the beans and cream.

- Stir well, cover and simmer for 2 minutes.

- Add the beans, stir to mix, then transfer the mixture to an ovenproof casserole dish.

- Cover and cook at 350°F/180°C for about 35–40 minutes.

- Add a little more water after 20 minutes, if necessary.

- Top each serving with a swirl of sour cream and serve immediately.

Serving suggestions: Serve with a mixed salad and crusty fresh bread, boiled rice or a baked potato.

Variations: Use cider vinegar in place of white wine vinegar. Use 4 leeks in place of the onions. Use other cooked beans such as flageolet or black-eyed beans in place of kidney beans.

COOK'S TIP

Canned kidney beans are ideal for this recipe and save you having to cook the beans yourself at home.

Red Bean Creole

A tempting bean and rice dish with a touch of heat. Cooking the dried beans in the microwave eliminates the need for overnight soaking.

Preparation time: 20 minutes · **Cooking time:** 1 hour 26 minutes (microwave), plus standing time · **Serves:** 4

¾ cup	dried red kidney beans	175 mL
2	bay leaves	2
	salt and freshly ground black pepper	
1⅔ cups	long-grain brown or white rice	400 mL
2 tbsp	butter or vegetable margarine	30 mL
2	green peppers, seeded and cut into thin strips	2
1 cup	mushrooms, sliced	250 mL
½ tsp	cayenne pepper	2 mL
½ tsp	ground nutmeg	2 mL
4	tomatoes, skinned, seeded and cut into strips	4
4	green onions, chopped	4
2 tbsp	chopped fresh parsley, to garnish	30 mL

• Cover the beans with water in a large microwave-proof bowl and cook in a microwave oven on HIGH for 10 minutes. Leave to stand for 1 hour, then drain and discard the liquid.

• Return the drained beans to the bowl and add the bay leaf, a little salt and pepper and enough fresh water to cover.

• Cover the bowl with plastic wrap and pierce several times with the tip of a sharp knife. Cook the beans on MEDIUM for 1 hour, then allow to stand for 10 minutes before draining completely. Set aside.

• Place the rice in another microwave-proof bowl with a little salt. Add 2½ cups (625 mL) cold water. Cook the rice on HIGH for 10 minutes. Leave to stand for 5 minutes, then drain and rinse in cold water. Set aside.

• Place the butter or margarine in a microwave-proof bowl and melt on HIGH for 30 seconds.

• Add the pepper and mushrooms and stir well to coat them evenly before cooking on HIGH for 2 minutes.

• Stir the pepper and mushrooms, then add the cayenne pepper, nutmeg, cooked rice and beans.

• Mix well, then cook on HIGH for 3 minutes, stirring once during the cooking time.

• Stir in the tomatoes and green onions and cook on HIGH for a further 1 minute before serving. Garnish with the chopped parsley.

Serving suggestions: Serve with herb-flavored bread or grilled mixed vegetables.

Variation: Use black-eyed or flageolet beans in place of kidney beans.

COOK'S TIP

Use 12 fl oz (341 mL) canned beans, drained, and omit steps 1–3 above for cooking your own beans.

Chana Masala

An excellent dish to serve hot as a main course, or cold as an accompaniment to a nut loaf.

Preparation time: 15 minutes · Cooking time: 30 minutes · Serves: 4

1	large onion, chopped	1
4	cloves of garlic, crushed	4
1	¾ -inch (20-mm) piece of fresh root ginger, finely chopped	1
¼ cup	clarified butter, margarine, or ghee	60 mL
4 tsp	ground coriander	20 mL
2 tsp	cumin seeds	10 mL
¼ tsp	cayenne pepper	1 mL
1 tsp	turmeric	5 mL
2 tsp	roasted cumin seeds, ground	10 mL
4 tsp	dried mango powder (amchur) or lemon juice	20 mL
2 tsp	paprika	10 mL
1	14-oz (398-mL) can of tomatoes	1
3½ cups	cooked (or canned) chickpeas	875 mL
1 tsp	garam masala	5 mL
	salt, to taste	
2	small fresh green chili peppers, finely chopped	2

• Cook the onion, garlic and ginger in the clarified butter, margarine or ghee in a pan until softened, stirring occasionally.

• Add all the spices, except the garam masala, and cook over a low heat for 1–2 minutes, stirring continuously.

• Add the tomatoes, roughly chopped, together with their juice.

• Add the cooked chickpeas and mix well.

• Cook for 30 minutes over a medium heat, stirring occasionally.

• Add the garam masala, salt and chilis, stir well and serve immediately.

Serving suggestions: Serve hot with boiled or pilau rice and mango chutney. This dish improves with time and is always more flavorful the following day.

Variations: Small pieces of diced vegetables such as potatoes, fresh tomatoes or cauliflower can be added to the dish at the start of cooking. Use cooked kidney or flageolet beans in place of chickpeas.

COOK'S TIP

Fry the spices over a low heat to ensure that they do not burn.

Quick Vegetable Chili

This popular, spicy dish is always a tasty treat.

Preparation time: 10 minutes · Cooking time: 25–30 minutes · Serves: 4

2	large onions, sliced	2
1 tbsp	olive oil	15 mL
1	clove of garlic, crushed	1
1 tsp	chili powder	5 mL
1	14-oz (398-mL) can of tomatoes, chopped	1
1	14-oz (398-mL) can of cooked red kidney beans	1
1	small red pepper, seeded and roughly chopped	1
1	medium zucchini, sliced into chunks	1
1 cup	cauliflower florets	250 mL
2	medium carrots, roughly chopped	2
2 tsp	tomato paste	10 mL
1 tsp	dried basil	5 mL
1 tsp	dried oregano	5 mL
1¼ cups	vegetable stock	300 mL
	fresh herb sprigs, to garnish	

• Sauté the onions in the oil in a pan until softened, stirring occasionally.

• Add the garlic and cook gently for 1 minute, stirring.

• Add the chili powder and cook gently for a further minute, stirring.

• Add the remaining ingredients, except the garnish, mix well and simmer for 25–30 minutes, stirring occasionally.

• Serve immediately, garnished with a sprig of fresh herb.

Serving suggestions: Serve with boiled brown or white rice, couscous or bulgur wheat.

Variations: Use broccoli in place of cauliflower, or sliced mushrooms. Use 4 leeks in place of the onion.

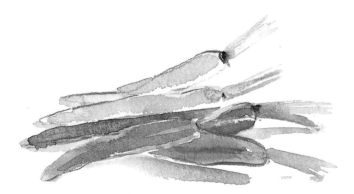

Mushroom Curry

This quick-and-easy, fragrant curry dish, laced with creamed coconut, is ideal for a suppertime treat.

Preparation time: 15 minutes · Cooking time: 20 minutes · Serves: 4–6

1 lb	leeks, thinly sliced	450 g
4	cloves of garlic, crushed	4
1 tsp	grated fresh ginger	5 mL
1½ tbsp	curry powder	25 mL
2 tsp	garam masala	10 mL
¼ cup	sunflower oil	60 mL
2¼ lbs	mushrooms, cut into quarters	1 kg
7 oz	creamed coconut, grated	200 g
2 tbsp	lemon juice	30 mL
	salt and freshly ground black pepper	
	fresh herb sprigs, to garnish	

• In a pan, fry the leeks, garlic, ginger and spices in the oil until soft, stirring frequently.

• Add the mushrooms and cook over a low heat until soft, stirring occasionally.

• Add the grated coconut and cook gently until the coconut has completely dissolved, adding a little water if the mixture appears too dry.

• Stir in the lemon juice and season with salt and pepper to taste. Serve hot, garnished with fresh herb sprigs.

Serving suggestion: Serve with boiled rice and a tomato and onion salad.

Variations: Use onions or shallots in place of leeks. Use lime juice in place of lemon juice.

Main Dishes with Pasta

Spaghetti with Pine Nuts

This crunchy, flavorsome combination makes good use of convenient ingredients often found in the cupboard.

Preparation time: 15 minutes · **Cooking time:** 25 minutes · **Serves:** 4

12 oz	spaghetti	350 g
1 tbsp	sunflower oil	15 mL
6 tbsp	olive oil	90 mL
1	large onion, sliced	1
1	clove of garlic, crushed	1
¼ cup	chopped fresh parsley	60 mL
1 cup	pine nuts	250 mL
1	14-oz (398-mL) can of artichoke hearts, drained and chopped	1
	salt and freshly ground black pepper	
½ cup	Cheddar cheese, grated (optional)	125 mL

• Cook the pasta in a large saucepan of lightly salted, boiling water with the sunflower oil added for 8–12 minutes, or until al dente. Drain and keep warm.

• Heat the olive oil in a frying pan. Add the onion and garlic and cook for 5 minutes, stirring occasionally.

• Add the parsley, pine nuts and artichokes and cook gently for 5 minutes, stirring occasionally.

• Stir in the cooked pasta and reheat gently, stirring occasionally. Season to taste with salt and pepper.

• Just before serving, stir in the grated cheese, if using, and serve immediately.

Serving suggestion: Serve with a mixed dark leaf side salad.

Variations: Use tagliatelle or fettuccine in place of spaghetti. Use Parmesan cheese in place of Cheddar. Use fresh basil in place of parsley.

Chinese Noodles with Vegetables

This is an Oriental-inspired vegetarian noodle dish. Chinese noodles are mixed with bamboo shoots, black mushrooms, cucumber and a light sauce consisting of a reduction of the cooking juices.

Preparation time: 40 minutes · Cooking time: 20 minutes · Serves: 4–6

2 tbsp	dried black Chinese mushrooms	30 mL
1	1-in (2.5-cm) piece of fresh ginger	1
1	clove of garlic	1
2	carrots	2
¼	cucumber	¼
8 oz	bamboo shoots	225 g
2 cups	bean sprouts	500 mL
14 oz	Chinese noodles	400 g
3 tbsp	olive oil	45 mL
1	small chili	1
5 tbsp	soy sauce	75 mL
1 tbsp	honey	15 mL
	salt and freshly ground black pepper	
	chopped fresh chives, to garnish	

• Soak the mushrooms in a bowl, covered with hot water, for 15 minutes. Trim off the sandy stumps, then boil the mushrooms in a saucepan of water for 5 minutes.

• Peel the ginger and garlic and finely chop. Set aside.

• Peel the carrots and cut into matchsticks. Squeeze out the water from the mushrooms and slice into matchsticks. Set aside.

• Peel and slice the cucumber into matchsticks. Set aside.

• Trim the bamboo shoots and cut into slices, then into matchsticks. Blanch in a pan of boiling water for 2 minutes. Set aside to drain thoroughly.

• Trim and wash the bean sprouts. Blanch for 1 minute in a pan of boiling water. Plunge into cold water and set aside to drain thoroughly.

• Cook the noodles in a pan of boiling, salted water for a few minutes, following the instructions on the packet. Drain, rinse and set aside to drain thoroughly.

• In a frying pan, heat the oil and fry the ginger, garlic and chili for 30 seconds, stirring.

• Add the bamboo shoots, mushrooms and carrots. Fry for 4 minutes, then add the bean sprouts. Cook for another 2 minutes, stirring occasionally.

• Add the noodles, soy sauce and honey. Stir well and cook until heated through, stirring.

• Add the cucumber and seasoning and heat for 1 minute, stirring. Remove and discard the chili. Serve immediately garnished with chopped chives.

Serving suggestion: Serve with fresh crusty bread or bread rolls.

Variations: Use sliced zucchinis in place of bean sprouts. Use parsnips in place of carrots.

Pasta with Fresh Basil Sauce

The fresh basil sauce in this recipe is made by pounding basil leaves with garlic, Parmesan cheese and olive oil using a pestle and mortar.

Preparation time: 25 minutes · Cooking time: 8 minutes · Serves: 4

1 lb	fresh pasta	454 g
20	fresh basil leaves	20
1	clove of garlic	1
2 tbsp	grated fresh Parmesan cheese	30 mL
¼ cup	olive oil	60 mL
2 tbsp	butter	30 mL
	salt and freshly ground black pepper	
	fresh basil sprigs, to garnish	

• Cook the pasta in salted, boiling water. Drain, rinse, then set aside to drain well.

• Pound the basil leaves with a mortar and pestle, then add the garlic and pound until well blended.

• Add the Parmesan cheese and continue to pound.

• Transfer the basil mixture to a large bowl, whisk in the olive oil, then set aside.

• Place cooked pasta in a large pan, add the butter and toss to mix. Place the pan over a gentle heat and add the basil sauce. Season with salt and pepper and heat through, stirring continuously with a wooden spoon. When hot, serve immediately garnished with basil sprigs.

Serving suggestion: Serve with a mixed leaf salad and slices of ciabatta rolls.

Variations: The sauce can be made in a food processor by adding all the ingredients together and processing until smooth. This reduces the preparation time to about 3 minutes. Sprinkle a handful of pine nuts over the pasta before serving, if you like.

Spaghetti with Zucchini Sauce

A flavorful vegetarian dish which is quick and very easy to prepare.

Preparation time: 20 minutes · Cooking time: 15 minutes · Serves: 2–4

10½ oz	spaghetti	300 g
5 tbsp	olive oil	75 mL
1	onion	1
2	cloves of garlic	2
3	medium zucchinis (total weight 1¼ lb/500 g)	3
2 tbsp	chopped fresh mixed herbs	30 mL
½ cup	heavy cream	125 mL
	salt and freshly ground black pepper	
1	beefsteak tomato, skinned	1

• Place the spaghetti in a saucepan of boiling salted water with 1 tbsp (15 mL) oil added, and cook for about 8–10 minutes, or until al dente, stirring occasionally with a fork. Drain well, set aside and keep warm.

• Meanwhile, to make the zucchini sauce, peel and thinly slice the onion and garlic, and slice the zucchinis into strips.

• Heat the remaining oil in a frying pan, add the onion, garlic and zucchinis and cook for about 3 minutes, stirring occasionally.

• Add the herbs and simmer for a further minute before adding the cream and salt and pepper.

• Cut the tomato into chunks and add to the pan. Heat through briefly until piping hot, stirring occasionally.

• Serve the hot spaghetti with the zucchini sauce spooned over the top.

Serving suggestion: Serve with thick slices of fresh wholewheat bread.

Variations: Use 2 leeks in place of the onion. Use mushrooms in place of all or half the zucchinis. Use 2 plum tomatoes in place of the beefsteak tomato. Sprinkle with grated Parmesan or Cheddar cheese just before serving, if you like.

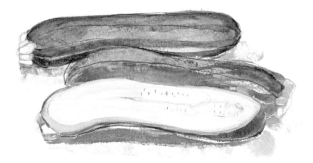

Conchiglie with Two Sauces

This exciting pasta recipe offers two contrasting vegetable sauces — tomato and mushroom — in a single dish.

Preparation time: 20 minutes · Cooking time: 30 minutes · Serves: 4

1 lb	cooked conchiglie (pasta shells)	450 g
	chopped fresh parsley, to garnish	
TOMATO SAUCE		
1	large onion, very finely chopped	1
1 tsp	bouillon or soup stock powder	5 mL
1	clove of garlic, crushed	1
½ tsp	dried thyme	2 mL
	a pinch of dried rosemary	
1	14-oz (398-mL) can of tomatoes	1
MUSHROOM SAUCE		
½ lb	oyster mushrooms	250 g
2 tbsp	butter	30 mL
1 tsp	bouillon or soup stock powder	5 mL
¼ cup	quark or low-fat cottage cheese	60 mL

• To make the tomato sauce, place the onion, bouillon powder, 3 tbsp (45 mL) water and garlic in a pan and cook very gently for 7–10 minutes, or until the onion is soft, stirring occasionally.

• Add the thyme and rosemary and cook for 1 minute, stirring.

• Chop the tomatoes and add to the pan together with the tomato juice.

• Bring to a boil and boil rapidly until the sauce has reduced and thickened, stirring occasionally.

• Meanwhile, to make the mushroom sauce, finely chop the mushrooms. Melt the butter in a pan and add the mushrooms and stock cube.

• Simmer very gently for 10 to 15 minutes, stirring occasionally. Remove from the heat and stir in the quark/cottage cheese. Heat gently until hot, but do not allow to boil.

• Divide the hot pasta between 4 serving dishes and pour the tomato sauce over one half of the pasta and the mushroom sauce over the other half of the pasta. Sprinkle the chopped parsley over the two sauces and serve at once.

Serving suggestion: Serve with a chopped mixed garden salad and fresh bread rolls.

Variations: Use button mushrooms in place of the oyster mushrooms. Use sour cream in place of quark/cottage cheese.

COOK'S TIP

The sauces can be prepared in advance, refrigerated and reheated thoroughly when required.

Hot Noodles

A gutsy Oriental-style noodle dish with mixed vegetables flavored with spices and chili sauce.

Preparation time: 15 minutes · Cooking time: 20 minutes · Serves: 4

8 oz	dried egg noodles	225 g
2 tbsp	vegetable oil	30 mL
1¼ cups	mushrooms, sliced	300 mL
1 cup	carrots, cut into matchsticks	250 mL
1	red pepper, seeded and cut into strips	1
½ lb	fresh bean sprouts	250 g
¼ lb	snow peas, trimmed	125 g
6	green onions, sliced into rings	6
1 tbsp	curry powder	15 mL
	a little ground cumin	
	salt	
1 tsp	Sambal Oelek (Oriental chili sauce)	5 mL
3 tbsp	soy sauce	45 mL

• Cook the noodles according to the instructions on the packet until just tender. Drain and keep warm.

• Heat the oil in a wok or large frying pan over a high heat. Add the mushrooms and stir-fry for 1 minute.

• Add the carrots, pepper and bean sprouts and stir-fry for 3 minutes.

• Add the snow peas and green onions and stir-fry for 1 minute.

• Season the vegetable mixture with the curry powder, cumin and salt to taste, then stir in the Sambal Oelek and soy sauce. Stir-fry for a further 1 minute.

• Add the noodles to the pan and stir until heated through. Serve immediately.

Serving suggestion: Serve with rice crackers.

Variations: Use oyster or shiitake mushrooms for added interest and variety. Use chopped bok choy in place of snow peas.

COOK'S TIP

For the best results, use a large wok and heat until smoking before adding the oil. Make sure the oil is very hot before adding the vegetables.

Spaghetti Pasty

An impressive wholewheat pasta pie, filled with a delicious carrot, mushroom and tofu mixture.

Preparation time: 45 minutes · Cooking time: 30–45 minutes · Serves: 4–6

10½ oz	wholewheat spaghetti	300 g
2¼ lb	carrots, sliced	1 kg
4	medium eggs, beaten	4
3 tbsp	sour cream	45 mL
3 tbsp	cornstarch	45 mL
1	clove of garlic, thinly sliced	1
2 tbsp	chopped fresh basil	30 mL
1–2 tbsp	soy sauce	15–30 mL
	salt and freshly ground black pepper	
2–3 tbsp	sunflower oil	30–45 mL
5 cups	button mushrooms	1.25 L
1 cup	tofu, cut into small cubes	250 mL
1⅔ cup	milk	400 mL
	ground nutmeg, to taste	
1¼ cups	Cheddar cheese, cubed or crumbled	300 mL
	fresh herbs sprigs, to garnish	

• Cook the spaghetti in a large pan of boiling salted water for about 15 minutes, or until al dente. Rinse with cold water, drain well, then lay out flat on a board so that the spaghetti does not stick together. Set aside.

• Meanwhile, steam the carrots over a pan of boiling water for about 30 minutes, until very tender. Purée the carrots in a food processor or blender until smooth.

• In a bowl, mix the carrots with 3 eggs, the sour cream and cornstarch. Stir the garlic into the mixture with the basil, soy sauce and salt and pepper to taste. Set aside.

• Meanwhile, heat 1 tbsp (15 mL) oil in a pan and fry the mushrooms with a little salt for about 5 minutes, until the liquid has evaporated, stirring occasionally.

• Add the mushrooms and tofu to the carrot mixture, stir well, then set aside.

• Beat the remaining egg, then coat the spaghetti thoroughly in the beaten egg.

• Line an ovenproof dish with cooking foil and brush with some of the remaining oil.

• Arrange some of the spaghetti on the dish in spirals against the edge of the dish. Spoon in the carrot mixture and press so that the spaghetti is held firmly in place against the sides of the dish. Top with the remaining spaghetti, then cover with cooking foil that has been coated with the remaining oil.

• Bake in a preheated oven at 425°F/220°C for 30–45 minutes, until cooked.

• When cooked, remove the foil, carefully remove the pasty from the dish and remove the foil from underneath it. Place on a serving plate and keep warm.

• Meanwhile, for the cheese sauce, pour the milk into a pan and season with salt and pepper and nutmeg. Add the cheese and cook gently, stirring continuously, until the sauce becomes creamy and is hot.

• Serve the spaghetti pasty with the cheese sauce alongside. Garnish with fresh herb sprigs.

●

Serving suggestion: Serve with cooked fresh vegetables such as green beans and corn.

Tortellini with Vegetables

Tender tortellini are tossed with a blue cheese and vegetable sauce to create this delectable dish.

Preparation time: 10 minutes · Cooking time: 15–20 minutes · Serves: 4

1 lb	dried tortellini, such as mixed cheese or spinach and ricotta	454 g
4 tbsp	butter	60 mL
8	green onions, chopped	8
¾ cup	heavy cream	175 mL
1 cup	Gorgonzola, or Blue cheese, crumbled	250 mL
¾ lb	snow peas, trimmed	350 g
12	cherry tomatoes	12
	salt and freshly ground black pepper	
4	sage leaves, finely chopped	4
4	shelled walnuts, chopped, for garnish	4

• Cook the tortellini in a large saucepan of lightly salted, boiling water until just cooked or al dente.

• Drain well, set aside and keep hot.

• Melt the butter in a pan, add the green onions and cook for 5 minutes, until softened, stirring occasionally.

• Pour the cream into the pan, then add the crumbled Gorgonzola to the pan, heating gently until the cheese has melted, stirring.

• Add the snow peas to the sauce and allow to cook for about 1 minute, stirring occasionally.

• Remove the stalks and cores from the tomatoes, add to the sauce and season with salt and pepper.

• Add the chopped sage leaf to the sauce and stir to mix.

• Add the cooked tortellini to the sauce and stir to mix.

• Reheat gently until hot, then serve immediately, garnished with chopped walnuts.

Serving suggestion: Serve with crusty French bread and a mixed leaf salad.

Variations: Use Stilton in place of Gorgonzola. Use sugar snap peas or sliced mushrooms in place of snow peas. Use sour cream in place of cream.

Penne with Roquefort Cream Sauce

The pasta tubes are tossed with a creamy cheese and mushroom sauce.

Preparation time: 10 minutes · Cooking time: 15–20 minutes · Serves: 4

½ lb	Roquefort cheese	225 g
2 cups	heavy cream	500 mL
	salt and freshly ground black pepper	
4 tbsp	butter	60 mL
½ lb	mushrooms, thinly sliced	225 g
14 oz	dried tricolor penne	400 g

• Crumble the Roquefort cheese and add to the cream in a pan. Mix well.

• Bring the cream mixture gently to a boil, stirring, and add salt and pepper to taste.

• Cook gently, stirring, until a creamy sauce has formed. Set aside and keep warm.

• Melt the butter in a pan, add the mushrooms and cook for about 5 minutes, stirring occasionally, until just cooked.

• Add salt and pepper to taste, set aside and keep warm.

• Meanwhile, cook the pasta in a saucepan of boiling salted water for 8–10 minutes, until just cooked or al dente.

• Drain the pasta thoroughly and return to the pan.

• Add the mushrooms and cream sauce and toss together to mix well. Serve hot.

Serving suggestion: Serve with crusty fresh bread and a mixed pepper and tomato salad.

Variations: Use Stilton or Blue cheese in place of Roquefort. Use sour cream in place of cream. Use zucchinis in place of mushrooms.

Main Dishes
au Gratin

Italian Vegetable Pie

The classic flavors of Italy are brought together in this delicious oven-baked vegetable dish.

Preparation time: 20 minutes · Cooking time: 25–30 minutes · Serves: 4

2	yellow peppers	2
2	red peppers	2
7 oz	Mozzarella cheese	200 g
4	medium zucchinis, sliced	4
⅓ cup	pitted black olives	75 mL
	salt and freshly ground black pepper	
2	cloves of garlic, crushed	2
2	bunches of fresh basil, chopped	2
6 tbsp	soya oil	90 mL

• Halve and seed the peppers, then slice into large strips.

• Place on a baking tray and bake in a preheated oven at 450°F/230°C until the skins are blackened.

• Place the pepper strips in a bowl, cover with a clean, damp tea-towel and when cool enough to handle, remove and discard the skins. Set aside.

• Slice the Mozzarella, then arrange the peppers, Mozzarella and zucchini slices in a greased ovenproof dish.

• Top with the olives and season with salt and pepper.

• In a small bowl or jug, mix the garlic and basil with the soya oil, then pour over the vegetables and cheese.

• Bake in the oven for 25–30 minutes, or until cooked and golden brown. Serve hot.

●

Serving suggestion: Serve with oven-baked potatoes and a fresh mixed garden salad.

Variations: Use Cheddar cheese in place of Mozzarella. Use chopped fresh coriander or chives in place of basil.

Potato and Zucchini Gratin

A quick and easy, yet rich and flavorsome baked dish.

Preparation time: 10 minutes · Cooking time: 20–25 minutes · Serves: 4

2 cups	cooked potatoes, sliced	500 mL
2 cups	zucchinis, sliced	500 mL
4	cloves of garlic, crushed	4
2 cups	heavy cream	500 mL
	freshly ground sea salt and black pepper	
2–4 tbsp	chopped fresh tarragon	30–60 mL
¾ cup	grated Emmenthal cheese	175 mL
	a knob of butter	

- Lay the potato and zucchini slices overlapping in a greased soufflé dish.

- In a bowl, mix the crushed garlic with the cream. Season to taste with salt and pepper.

- Stir in the chopped tarragon, then pour the mixture evenly over the vegetables.

- Sprinkle over the grated cheese and dot with the butter.

- Bake in a preheated oven at 425°F/220°C for 20–25 minutes, until cooked and golden brown. Serve hot.

Serving suggestion: Serve with a crisp green salad and crusty French bread or Italian ciabatta rolls.

Variations: Use sweet potatoes in place of standard potatoes. Use mushrooms in place of zucchinis. Use Cheddar cheese in place of Emmenthal. Use fresh basil or parsley in place of tarragon.

Baked Broccoli

Fresh broccoli florets and mushrooms are mildly spiced, topped with cheese and a creamy sauce and baked in the oven to perfection.

Preparation time: 20 minutes · Cooking time: 20 minutes · Serves: 4

3½ cups	broccoli florets	875 mL
¼ cup	vegetable oil	60 mL
2½ cups	brown mushrooms, halved or sliced	625 mL
¾ cup	red onions, sliced	175 mL
	salt and freshly ground black pepper	
	ground turmeric	
	ground cumin	
2 tbsp	toasted sesame seeds	30 mL
1½ cups	grated Emmenthal cheese	375 mL
SAUCE		
4 tsp	toasted sesame seeds	20 mL
1 cup	heavy cream	250 mL
4 tsp	sour cream	20 mL
	salt and freshly ground black pepper	

• Cook the broccoli in a saucepan of lightly salted, boiling water for about 5 minutes, until just tender. Drain well and set aside.

• Heat the oil in a pan and cook the mushrooms and onions for 3 minutes, stirring. Remove the pan from the heat and stir in the broccoli.

• Arrange the mixed vegetables in an oval ovenproof dish and season to taste with salt and pepper, turmeric and cumin.

• Sprinkle over the sesame seeds and cheese.

• For the sauce, mix the sesame seeds with the cream and sour cream and season with salt and pepper.

• Pour the sauce over the vegetables. Bake in a preheated oven at 400°F/200°C for 20 minutes, until golden brown and bubbling. Serve hot.

Serving suggestion: Serve with boiled rice or pasta and fresh crusty bread.

Variations: Use curry powder or ground coriander in place of cumin. Use cauliflower in place of broccoli.

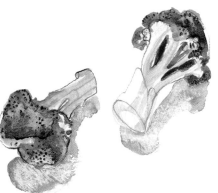

203

Chinese Cabbage Gratin

A delicious cheese-topped mixed vegetable bake.

Preparation time: 20 minutes · Cooking time: 30 minutes · Serves: 4

1	Chinese cabbage (napa) 1½ lb/750 g	1
2½ cups	mushrooms, sliced	625 mL
	salt and freshly ground black pepper	
⅔ cup	sour cream	150 mL
⅔ cup	rich plain yogurt	150 mL
2	eggs	2
	grated nutmeg, to taste	
	curry powder, to taste	
¾ cup	grated Gouda cheese	175 mL

• Cut the Chinese cabbage into four and rinse thoroughly. Cook in a saucepan of salted boiling water for about 6 minutes.

• Drain the cabbage, then place it in a greased ovenproof dish.

• Lay the mushroom slices over the cabbage and season to taste with salt and pepper.

• In a bowl, mix the sour cream and yogurt together, beat in the eggs and season with salt and pepper.

• Add grated nutmeg and curry powder, stir well, then pour the sauce over the mushrooms.

• Sprinkle with the grated cheese and cook in a preheated oven at 400°F/200°C for about 30 minutes, until golden brown. Serve hot.

Serving suggestions: Serve with a mixed leaf salad or baked potatoes.

Variations: Use zucchinis in place of mushrooms. Use Cheddar cheese in place of Gouda. Use green cabbage in place of Chinese cabbage.

Root Vegetable Risotto with Snow Peas

A delicious oven-baked risotto — ideal for warming those chilly evenings.

Preparation time: 40 minutes · Cooking time: 20 minutes · Serves: 4

2 tbsp	olive oil	30 mL
¾ cup	long-grain rice	175 mL
1⅔ cups	vegetable stock	400 mL
	salt and freshly ground black pepper	
4	eggs	4
1 cup	heavy cream	250 mL
⅔ cup	low-fat cottage cheese	150 mL
	grated nutmeg	
1⅔ lb	mixed root vegetables such as parsnips, rutabagas, turnips and carrots, diced	750 g
1½ cups	snow peas, trimmed	375 mL
1	bunch of fresh flat-leafed parsley	1
½ cup	grated Parmesan cheese	125 mL
3 tbsp	butter flakes	45 mL
	fresh herb sprigs, to garnish	

• Heat the oil in a pan, add the rice and cook for 1 minute, stirring. Add the vegetable stock and season with salt and pepper.

• Bring to a boil, then reduce the heat and simmer, uncovered, for 15–18 minutes, until all the liquid has been absorbed, stirring gently. Remove the pan from the heat and set aside.

• Beat the eggs in a bowl, add the cream and cottage cheese and mix well. Season to taste with salt and pepper and grated nutmeg.

• Cook the root vegetables in a pan of boiling water for 8–10 minutes, or until cooked and tender. Drain, mash and set aside.

• Blanch the snow peas for 3 minutes in a saucepan of boiling water, then remove, drain and mix with the mashed vegetables.

• Finely chop the parsley. Grease an ovenproof dish, then fill with layers of the rice and mixed vegetables, ending with a layer of vegetables. Season each layer with salt and pepper and sprinkle with chopped parsley.

• Pour the egg and cream mixture evenly over the top of the vegetables. Cover with cheese, dot with the butter flakes and bake in a preheated oven at 400°F/200°C for about 20 minutes, or until cooked and golden brown.

• Garnish with fresh herb sprigs and serve immediately.

Serving suggestions: Serve with a mixed dark leaf salad or a mixed pepper, tomato and onion salad.

Variations: Use sugar-snap peas or sliced mushrooms or zucchinis in place of snow peas. Use chopped fresh coriander in place of parsley.

Savory Rice Cake

This is an excellent way to use up leftover rice.

Preparation time: 15 minutes · Cooking time: 15 minutes · Serves: 4

2	onions, finely chopped	2
2	cloves of garlic, crushed	2
¼ cup	olive oil	60 mL
2 tbsp	chopped fresh thyme	30 mL
2	red peppers, seeded and thinly sliced	2
2	green peppers, seeded and thinly sliced	2
8	eggs, beaten	8
	salt and freshly ground black pepper	
¾ cup	cooked brown rice	175 mL
6 tbsp	plain yogurt	90 mL
1½ cups	grated Cheddar cheese	375ml
	fresh thyme sprigs, to garnish	

- In a frying pan, fry the onion and garlic in the oil until soft.

- Add the chopped thyme and peppers and fry gently for 4–5 minutes, stirring occasionally.

- In a bowl, beat the eggs with salt and pepper to taste.

- Add the cooked rice to the thyme and peppers followed by the eggs.

- Cook over a moderate heat, stirring from time to time, until the eggs are cooked underneath.

- Spoon the yogurt on top of the partly set egg mixture and sprinkle the cheese over the top.

- Place under a preheated broiler and cook until puffed and golden. Serve immediately, garnished with fresh thyme sprigs.

Serving suggestions: Serve with a mixed green salad and warmed bread rolls, or cooked green vegetables and boiled potatoes.

Variations: Use a mixture of cooked brown and wild rice, for a change. Use chopped fresh sage, oregano or marjoram in place of thyme.

Macaroni and Cheese with Apple

The classic combination of apples and Cheddar cheese makes this variation on macaroni and cheese something quite out of the ordinary—and it's a quick and easy dish cooked in the microwave.

Preparation time: 15 minutes · Cooking time: 23 minutes (microwave on HIGH) · Serves: 4–6

3 cups	wholewheat macaroni	750 mL
4 tsp	vegetable oil	20 mL
2½ cups	milk	625 mL
2 tbsp	butter or vegetable margarine	30 mL
2 tbsp	wholewheat flour	30 mL
2 tbsp	arrowroot	30 mL
1 tsp	dried tarragon	5 mL
	a pinch of salt	
2 cups	crumbled or grated Cheddar cheese	500 mL
2	apples, peeled, quartered, cored and chopped	2
2	onions, chopped	2
2	cloves of garlic, crushed	2
	fresh herb sprigs, to garnish	

• Place the macaroni in a microwave-proof bowl along with 2 tsp (10 mL) oil and enough boiling water to cover. Cook in a microwave oven on HIGH for 10 minutes, or until the pasta is just cooked or al dente.

• Drain the pasta and rinse in cold water to prevent it from becoming soggy. Set aside.

• Combine the milk, butter or margarine, flour, arrowroot, tarragon and salt in a small microwave-proof bowl and mix well.

• Cook on HIGH for 2 minutes. Stir well, then cook again for a further 2 minutes on HIGH.

• Reserve ½ cup (125 mL) cheese for the topping. Stir the remaining cheese into the sauce mixture and cook on HIGH for 1 minute, to melt the cheese. Set aside.

• Place the apple, onion, garlic and remaining 2 tsp (10 mL) oil into a large microwave-proof bowl and mix well to coat the ingredients thoroughly in the oil.

• Cover the bowl with plastic wrap and pierce several times with the tip of a sharp knife.

• Cook the apple and onion mixture on HIGH for 3–4 minutes, to soften.

• Stir the cheese sauce into the apple and onion mixture, then stir in the drained pasta.

• Transfer to a serving dish and sprinkle the reserved cheese over the top. Cook on HIGH for 4 minutes to heat through and melt the topping. Serve immediately, garnished with fresh herb sprigs.

Serving suggestion: Serve with a mixed leaf side salad.

Variation: Use dried sage in place of tarragon.

Lentil Moussaka

Sample the flavors of the Greek islands with this classic, popular dish.

Preparation time: 1 hour · Cooking time: 40 minutes · Serves: 4–6

¾ cup	whole green lentils	175 mL
1	large eggplant, sliced	1
4–5 tbsp	olive oil	60–75 mL
1	large onion, chopped	1
1	clove of garlic, crushed	1
1	large carrot, diced	1
4	sticks of celery, finely chopped	4
1–2 tsp	dried mixed herbs	5–10 mL
1	14-oz (398-mL) can of chopped tomatoes	1
2 tsp	shoyu (Japanese soy sauce)	10 mL
	freshly ground black pepper, to taste	
2	medium potatoes, cooked and sliced	2
2	large tomatoes, sliced	2
SAUCE		
4 tbsp	vegetable margarine	60 mL
½ cup	brown rice flour	125 mL
1¾ cups	milk	425 mL
1	large egg, separated	1
½ cup	grated Cheddar cheese	125 mL
1 tsp	ground nutmeg	5 mL
	fresh herb sprigs, to garnish	

• Cook the lentils in plenty of water in a saucepan until soft. Drain and reserve the liquid and lentils separately.

• Meanwhile, fry the eggplant in the oil in a pan until lightly browned. Drain well and set aside.

• Sauté the onion, garlic, carrot, celery and a little of the lentil stock in a pan.

• Simmer with the lid on until just tender, stirring occasionally.

• Add the lentils, mixed herbs and canned tomatoes. Simmer gently for 3–4 minutes. Season with shoyu and pepper.

• Place a layer of the lentil mixture in a large casserole dish and cover with half the eggplant slices.

• Cover the eggplant slices with half the potato slices and all the tomato slices.

• Repeat with the remaining lentils, eggplants and potatoes.

• For the sauce, melt the margarine in a saucepan, remove from the heat and stir in the flour to form a roux. Add the milk gradually, blending well so that the sauce is smooth.

• Return to the heat and stir continuously until the sauce thickens.

• Remove the pan from the heat and cool slightly. Add the egg yolk, stir in the cheese and add the nutmeg.

• Whisk the egg white in a bowl until stiff, then carefully fold into the sauce.

• Pour the sauce over the moussaka, covering the dish completely. Bake in a preheated oven at 350°F/180°C for about 40 minutes, until the top is golden brown and puffy. Serve hot, garnished with fresh herb sprigs.

●

Serving suggestion: Serve with a crunchy green salad.

Variations: Use whole brown lentils in place of green. Use sweet potatoes in place of standard potatoes.

Ratatouille Lasagne

An appetizing Mediterranean vegetable lasagne — a satisfying choice for lunch or supper.

Preparation time: 30 minutes · Cooking time: 35 minutes · Serves: 4–6

6	strips of lasagne verde or wholewheat lasagne	6
2–3 tbsp	olive oil	30–45 mL
2	onions, finely chopped	2
2	cloves of garlic, crushed	2
2	large eggplants, chopped	2
1	medium zucchini, thinly sliced	1
1	green pepper, seeded and chopped	1
1	red pepper, seeded and chopped	1
1	14-oz (398-mL) can of chopped tomatoes	1
2–3 tbsp	tomato paste	30–45 mL
	a little vegetable stock	
	salt and freshly ground black pepper	

WHITE SAUCE

2 tbsp	butter	30 mL
¼ cup	plain wholewheat flour	60 mL
1¼ cups	milk	300 mL
½ cup	grated Parmesan cheese	125 mL
	fresh parsley sprigs, to garnish	

• Cook the lasagne in boiling, salted water for 12–15 minutes. Plunge into a bowl of cold water to prevent overcooking or sticking.

• Heat the oil in a frying pan and fry the onion and garlic until soft.

• Add the eggplant, zucchini and peppers and cook until soft, stirring occasionally.

• Add the tomatoes with their juice and the tomato paste and simmer until tender, stirring occasionally. It may be necessary to add a little stock at this stage. Season well and set aside.

• Make the white sauce by melting the butter in a small saucepan. Add the flour and cook for 1 minute, stirring.

• Add the milk slowly, stirring constantly, bring to a boil and simmer for about 3 minutes. Remove from the heat.

• Grease a deep ovenproof dish. Layer the ratatouille and lasagne strips, starting with the ratatouille and finishing with a layer of lasagne.

• Pour on the white sauce and sprinkle the Parmesan cheese over the top.

• Bake in a preheated oven at 350°F/180°C for about 35 minutes, until golden brown and bubbling. Garnish with parsley sprigs before serving. Serve hot.

Serving suggestion: Serve with crusty bread rolls and a green salad.

Variations: If eggplant is not available, use 3 cups (750 mL) sliced mushrooms instead. Use 3 cups (750 mL) fresh tomatoes, skinned and chopped, in place of canned tomatoes. Use 3–4 leeks in place of onions.

Beany Lasagne

This tasty lasagne is suitable for a family meal or for entertaining friends.

Preparation time: 35 minutes · Cooking time: 35 minutes · Serves: 4–6

8	strips of wholewheat lasagne	8
1	large onion, finely chopped	1
1 tbsp	vegetable oil	15 mL
	salt	
1–2	cloves of garlic, crushed	1–2
1 cup	cooked aduki beans	250 mL
1	green pepper, seeded and chopped	1
1	14-oz (398-mL) can of chopped tomatoes	1
1 tbsp	tomato paste	15 mL
1 tsp	dried basil	5 mL
1 tsp	dried oregano	5 mL
	shoyu (Japanese soy sauce) or salt	
	freshly ground black pepper	
SAUCE		
2 tbsp	butter or vegetable margarine	30 mL
¼ cup	plain wholewheat flour	60 mL
1¾ cups	cold dairy or soya milk	425 mL
½ cup	grated Cheddar cheese (optional)	125 mL
	fresh herb sprigs, to garnish	

• Cook the lasagne in a large pan of boiling salted water for 8–10 minutes, until al dente. Drain well and drape over a cooling rack or the sides of a colander to cool and prevent sticking together.

• Meanwhile, in a pan, soften the onion in the oil, sprinkling with a little salt to draw out the juice, then add the garlic.

• Add the beans, pepper, tomatoes, tomato paste and dried herbs and stir to mix.

• Simmer for about 10 minutes, or until the vegetables are tender, stirring occasionally.

• Stir in the shoyu and season to taste.

• Meanwhile, for the sauce, combine the margarine or butter, flour and milk in a pan. Gradually bring to a boil, whisking continuously.

• When thickened, allow to simmer, partly covered, for about 6 minutes, stirring frequently.

• Stir the cheese, if using, into the sauce and season.

• Layer the lasagne in a greased dish in the following order: half the bean mix, half the pasta, the remainder of the bean mix, then the remainder of the pasta. Top with the sauce.

• Bake in a preheated oven at 350°F/180°C for about 35 minutes, or until golden brown and bubbling.

• Serve in the dish in which it has been cooked and garnish with fresh herb sprigs.

Serving suggestion: Serve with a green salad and crusty fresh bread.

Variations: Use lasagne verde in place of wholewheat lasagne. Use other cooked beans such as black-eye or flageolet in place of aduki beans.

Desserts and Breads

Auckland Fruit Salad

A luscious fruit combination topped with a dreamy liqueur-laced cream.

Preparation time: 20 minutes, plus 30 minutes standing time · Serves: 4

3	kiwi fruits	3
2	dessert pears	2
2½ cups	strawberries	625 mL
2 cups	grapes	500 mL
	juice of 2 lemons	
2 tbsp	Cointreau	30 mL
3 tbsp	sugar	45 mL
½ cup	sour cream	125 mL
¼ cup	Irish cream liqueur	60 mL
1 tsp	brown sugar	5 mL

• Peel the kiwi fruit, cut in half lengthwise, then slice the flesh. Place in a large bowl.

• Peel the pears, then cut into quarters, remove and discard the cores and slice the flesh. Add to the bowl.

• Halve or quarter the strawberries if large and add to the bowl.

• Cut the grapes in half and remove and discard the seeds. Add to the other fruit.

• Gently mix the fruit with the lemon juice, Cointreau and sugar. Set aside for about 30 minutes for the flavors to develop.

• For the dressing, in a small bowl, mix the sour cream with the Irish cream liqueur and brown sugar.

• Serve the fruit salad in individual dishes with the Irish cream sauce spooned over or served separately.

Serving suggestion: Serve with wafer roll cookies.

Variations: Use apples in place of pears. Use Grand Marnier in place of Cointreau. Use heavy cream or plain yogurt in place of sour cream.

Exotic Fruit Salad

Mangoes have a distinctively fragrant flavor, giving this beautiful fruit salad a natural tangy sweetness.

Preparation time: 25 minutes, plus 1 hour chiling time · Serves: 4–6

3	ripe peaches	3
3	kiwi fruits	3
1	large star fruit	1
1 cup	fresh strawberries	250 mL
2	well-ripened mangoes, ¾ lb/350 g each	2
	juice of ½ lime	
¾ cup	red currants	175 mL
	a few strawberry leaves, to decorate	

• Plunge the peaches into boiling water for a few seconds, then carefully peel away the skin using a sharp knife.

• Cut the peaches in half and remove and discard the pits.

• Cut the peach halves into thin slices, then arrange on a serving plate.

• Peel the kiwi fruit, then slice crosswise.

• Trim away any dark pieces from the skin of the star fruit, then thinly slice the flesh and remove any small seeds.

• Leave the green tops on the strawberries and cut in half lengthwise.

• Arrange all the remaining prepared fruit on the serving plate with the peaches.

• Peel the mango and chop away the flesh from the large inner pit. Place in a food processor or juicer with the lime juice and half the red currants.

• Purée the mixture until smooth, then press through a nylon sieve to remove the red currant skins and seeds.

• Remove any hard stems or leaves from the remaining red currants and scatter over the fruit salad.

• Pour the fruit purée evenly over the salad, and chill for at least 1 hour before serving. Serve, decorated with strawberry leaves.

Serving suggestion: Serve with ginger snaps.

Variations: Use your own choice of fruits for the fruit salad, but do not substitute the mango. Use lemon juice in place of lime juice.

COOK'S TIP

If you do not have a food processor or juicer, a really ripe mango will rub easily through a wire sieve.

Fresh Fruit in Red Wine Syrup

A lovely summery dessert with a spicy red wine sauce. Use as many different kinds of fresh fruit as you can.

Preparation time: 20 minutes, depending on the type of fruit used, plus chilling time · Cooking time: 30 minutes · Serves: 8

4 cups	red wine (Beaujolais or similar)	1 L
2¼ cups	sugar	550 mL
1	whole clove	1
	finely grated rind of 1 orange	
1	stick of cinnamon	1
8 cups	a selection of fresh fruit, peeled, pitted, sliced or halved as necessary	2 L
	fresh mint leaves, to garnish	

• For the syrup, place the wine, ¾ cup (175 mL) water, sugar, clove, orange rind and cinnamon in a pan and boil for at least 30 minutes.

• Remove from the heat and set aside to cool. Chill in the refrigerator.

• Prepare the fruit, place in a serving dish and gently mix together.

• Remove the clove and cinnamon from the syrup, then pour over the fruit and serve, garnished with mint leaves.

Serving suggestions: Serve with scoops of orange sorbet or vanilla ice cream.

Variations: Once the syrup has chilled, add the fruit and marinate for 1 day in the refrigerator before serving. Use a bruised cardamom pod in place of the clove.

COOK'S TIP

Use only very fresh fruit for this dish.

Melon Salad

A simple, fresh-tasting dessert with a tangy lemon and honey dressing topped with crunchy hazelnuts.

Preparation time: 15 minutes · Serves: 4

1	honeydew melon, weighing about 1¼ lb (500 g)	1
2	dessert apples	2
2	bananas	2
1 cup	mandarin orange segments	250 mL
2–3 tbsp	lemon juice	30–45 mL
2 tbsp	honey	30 mL
	chopped hazelnuts	

• Cut the melon in quarters, remove and discard the seeds, then peel. Cut the flesh into strips.

• Peel the apples and cut into quarters. Remove and discard the cores, then cut the apples into strips.

• Peel the bananas and thinly slice.

• Place the prepared fruit in a serving bowl with the mandarin orange segments.

• Add the lemon juice and honey and mix thoroughly.

• Sprinkle with the chopped hazelnuts and serve.

●

Serving suggestions: For a special occasion, serve the fruit salad in a chilled melon half, with 'V' shapes cut from around the edge of the fruit. Serve with thick cream or ice cream.

Variations: Use dessert pears in place of apples. Use walnuts or almonds in place of hazelnuts.

Fresh and Dried Fruit Salad

Perk up dried fruit with fresh seasonal varieties — apples and oranges in winter and soft fruits or peaches in summer.

Preparation time: 10 minutes · Cooking time: 8 minutes (microwave) · Serves: 4

½ lb	mixed dried fruit (apples, apricots, raisins, mango, pineapple, etc.)	225 g
1 cup	apple juice	250 mL
2	apples	2
1	orange	1

• Combine the dried fruit and apple juice in a microwave-proof bowl.

• Cook in a microwave oven on MEDIUM for 8 minutes. Set aside to cool.

• Core and chop the apples, leaving the skins on.

• Peel the orange and remove all the white pith. Cut the flesh away from the thin membranes, then cut into pieces.

• In a bowl, mix together the chopped apples, oranges, dried fruit and apple juice. Chill until required.

• To serve, spoon the fruit salad into individual dishes.

●

Serving suggestions: For a low-fat dessert, serve with low-fat plain yogurt or low-fat cottage cheese. Alternatively, serve with plain yogurt or cream.

Variations: Use any dried fruit of your choice for this recipe. Use orange juice in place of apple juice. Use dessert pears in place of apples. Use 2 mandarin oranges in place of the orange.

Baked Raspberry Apples

A delicious fruity combination, perfectly complemented by cream or yogurt.

Preparation time: 10 minutes · Cooking time: 30–35 minutes · Serves: 4

2 tbsp	concentrated apple juice	30 mL
2 tbsp	honey	30 mL
1 tsp	ground mixed spice	5 mL
2	large apples	2
2 cups	fresh raspberries	500 mL

• Place the apple juice, ¼ cup (60 mL) water, honey and mixed spice in a large bowl and mix together well.

• Using a sharp knife, make deep zig-zag cuts around the apples.

• Take one half of the apple in each hand and twist gently in opposite directions until the 2 halves come apart.

• Remove and discard the core and immerse the apple halves in the apple juice mixture.

• Place the apple halves in an oven-proof dish and bake in a preheated oven at 400°F/200°C for 20 to 25 minutes, until just soft. Reduce oven temperature to 300°F/150°C.

• Remove from the oven and top with the raspberries.

• Pour the remaining apple juice mixture over the raspberries and return to the oven for 10 minutes. Serve at once.

Serving suggestions: Serve topped with a spoonful of plain yogurt or whipped cream.

Variations: Use fresh blackberries or small strawberries in place of raspberries. Use concentrated orange juice or pineapple juice in place of apple juice. Use ground ginger or cinnamon in place of mixed spice.

COOK'S TIP

Frozen raspberries can be used for this recipe, but make sure they are well thawed before using.

Melon with Caramelized Orange Peel

This fruity dessert is laced with wine and Cointreau and sweetened with honey.

Preparation time: 20 minutes · Cooking time: 10 minutes · Serves: 4

4	honeydew, galias or cantaloupe melons	4
4	oranges	4
1 cup	white wine	250 mL
¼ cup	honey	60 mL
¼ cup	Cointreau	60 mL
4	medium egg whites	4
¼ cup	icing sugar, sifted	60 mL

• Cut the melons in half, remove and discard the seeds, then remove the flesh from one half of each melon using a melon baller. Place the melon balls in a bowl.

• Place the remaining melon halves in the refrigerator.

• Peel the oranges very thinly, then thinly slice the peel into strips.

• Mix the wine and honey in a pan, add the orange peel and cook until all the liquid is evaporated and the peel is caramelized, stirring frequently. Remove from the heat and set aside.

• Remove all the pith from the peeled oranges and divide into segments.

• Chop the orange segments, then mix with the caramelized orange peel and melon balls.

• Dissolve the remaining caramel in the pan with the Cointreau.

• Pile the mixed fruit into the chilled melon half and return to the refrigerator to chill for 1 hour.

• In a bowl, whisk the egg whites and icing sugar together until stiff.

• Place the mixture in an icing bag fitted with a star nozzle and pipe rosettes on top of the chilled melon so that all the fruit is covered.

• Place under a preheated grill and cook for about 3 minutes until the meringue mixture is lightly browned. Serve immediately.

Serving suggestion: Serve with fresh whipped cream or thick-set plain yogurt.

Variations: Use 4 small red grapefruits (or 2 medium-size) in place of the oranges. Use rosé wine in place of white wine.

Fruit Salad Trifle

A sumptuous trifle of mixed fruits and nuts with a light carob sponge cake base and a yogurt-cream topping — ideal for entertaining.

Preparation time: 30 minutes, plus cooling and chilling time · Cooking time: 20 minutes · Serves: 6

CAROB SPONGE CAKE

½ cup	soft butter or margarine	125 mL
½ cup	light brown sugar	125 mL
2	medium eggs	2
¾ cup	plain wholewheat flour, sifted	175 mL
¼ cup	carob powder	60 mL
1½ tsp	baking powder	7.5 mL

TRIFLE

6 tbsp	apple juice	90 mL
1–2 tbsp	apricot or banana liqueur (optional)	15–30 mL
2	crisp apples, cored and chopped but not peeled	2
1	large banana, sliced	1
2	oranges, segmented and roughly chopped	2
	half a pineapple, cored and diced	
	a few grapes, halved and seeded	
½ cup	dates, pitted and chopped	125 mL
½ cup	hazelnuts, chopped	125 mL
½ cup	whipping cream	125 mL
½ cup	plain yogurt	125 mL
	orange segments, pineapple cubes and carob chips, to decorate	

COOK'S TIP

Since this recipe makes two halves of sponge and only one is needed for the trifle, the other half can be frozen or used on a subsequent occasion.

• Cream the margarine and sugar together in a bowl until pale and fluffy.

• Beat in the eggs one at a time, then carefully fold in the flour, carob powder and baking powder.

• Turn into 2 greased 7-in (18-cm) cake pans, and level the surfaces. Bake in a preheated oven at 350°F/180°C for about 20 minutes, until golden brown and risen.

• Turn out onto a wire rack to cool. Set aside.

• Place one of the carob cakes into a glass bowl and saturate with the apple juice. Set aside for 30 minutes.

• Add the liqueur, if using, then arrange the prepared fruits and nuts over the cake, covering it completely.

• In a bowl, whip the cream until stiff, then fold in the yogurt.

• Spread evenly over the fruit, covering it completely.

• With the back of a fork, trace from the rim of the bowl into the center, making a lined pattern. Chill before serving. Decorate with orange segments, pineapple cubes and carob chips and serve.

Serving suggestion: Trifle is best served on its own or with a little extra cream or yogurt.

Variations: Use your own choice of fresh prepared fruit for this trifle. Use cocoa powder in place of carob powder. Use plain white flour in place of wholewheat flour. Use almonds or pistachio nuts in place of hazelnuts.

Brandied Oranges with Peach and Mango Cream

An attractive, elegant dessert which tastes as good as it looks.

Preparation time: 20 minutes, plus chilling time · Cooking time: 2 minutes · Serves: 4

6	large oranges	6
3 tbsp	brandy	45 mL
2	mangoes, peeled, pitted and cut into chunks	2
4	small ripe peaches, peeled, pitted and roughly chopped	4
3 tbsp	heavy cream	45 mL

• Finely pare the outer rind (zest) from 3 of the oranges and boil the zest in a little water in a pan for 2 minutes.

• Remove from the heat, drain and cool.

• Peel the oranges using a sharp knife, making sure that all the pith is removed.

• Thinly slice the oranges, arrange in a serving dish and sprinkle the zest over the top.

• Sprinkle the brandy over the oranges, cover and refrigerate for about 1 hour.

• Place the mangos and peaches in a food processor or blender and blend until smooth. Place in a bowl.

• Stir in the cream, cover and refrigerate until required.

• Serve the oranges with the peach and mango cream alongside.

Serving suggestion: Serve with square wafers or wafer roll cookies.

Variations: Use plain yogurt or sour cream in place of heavy cream. Use nectarines in place of peaches. Use pink or ruby grapefruit in place of oranges.

COOK'S TIP

Use a zester to remove the zest from the oranges.

Fruit Kebabs with Mango Topping

These luscious kebabs will bring an exotic dimension to your dinner table.

Preparation time: 25 minutes · Cooking time: 15 minutes · Serves: 4

2	fresh figs	2
1	papaya	1
1	small pineapple	1
4	small mangoes	4
2	small oranges	2
2	kiwis	2
8	kumquats	8
3 tbsp	butter	45 mL
3½ tbsp	honey	50 mL
2 tbsp	lime juice	30 mL
¼ cup	orange juice	60 mL
1 cup	finely chopped or ground almonds	250 mL
½ cup	sugar	125 mL
4	egg yolks	4
3½ tbsp	unsweetened apple juice	50 mL
2 tbsp	lemon juice	30 mL

• Top and tail the figs, then cut into quarters. Set aside. Peel the papaya and remove and discard the seeds. Cut the flesh into thick slices, then cut in half crosswise.

• Peel the pineapple, then cut into slices, removing and discarding the woody core. Set aside. Peel and pit two mangoes, slice the flesh into thick segments, then cut in half crosswise.

• Peel the oranges and break into segments. Peel the kiwis and cut into 8 pieces. Set aside.

• Spear all the prepared fruit onto 8 short or 4 long skewers, dividing the ingredients equally between each skewer, adding the kumquats onto the ends to hold the other ingredients in place. Set aside.

• For the sauce, melt the butter in a saucepan with the honey over a low heat. Add the lime juice and orange juice and stir until a thick sauce has formed.

• Spoon the sauce over the kebabs and sprinkle with the flaked or ground almonds.

• Cook under a preheated medium grill at its closest position for 8–10 minutes, turning the kebabs frequently.

• Meanwhile, for the mango topping, peel the remaining mangoes, remove and discard the pit, then purée the flesh in a blender or food processor until smooth.

• Place in a bowl. Stir in the sugar, egg yolks, apple juice and lemon juice and mix well.

• Place the bowl over a pan of simmering water and beat until thickened.

• Serve the hot kebabs immediately, topped with the mango sauce.

⬤

Serving suggestions: Serve with ice cream, yogurt or cream.

Variations: Use your own choice of fruit, or what is available. Use finely chopped or ground hazelnuts in place of almonds.

Blueberry Pancakes

Pancakes are always a joy to eat, and this blueberry version is particularly delicious.

Preparation time: 10 minutes, plus 10 minutes standing time · Cooking time: 8–10 minutes · Serves: 4

6 tbsp	plain flour	90 mL
1 cup	milk	250 mL
½ tsp	salt	2 mL
4	eggs	4
½ tsp	baking powder	2 mL
6 tbsp	butter	90 mL
¾–1 cup	blueberries	175–250 mL
	sugar, to taste	
	fresh mint sprigs, to decorate	

• In a bowl, beat the flour, milk and salt together with a whisk until smooth.

• Leave the mixture to stand for about 10 minutes, then beat the eggs and baking powder into the batter, mixing well.

• Melt about 2 tsp (10 mL) of the butter in a small frying or omelette pan, then pour in ¼ of the batter, covering the base of the pan completely. Spread a quarter of the blueberries evenly over the mixture.

• Cook for about 4 minutes, then slide the pancake out onto a large plate to turn it.

• Add another 2 tsp (10 mL) of butter to the pan and heat until melted.

• Return the pancake to the pan, with the uncooked side of the pancake face down in the pan, and cook for a further 4–5 minutes until brown. Put in a warming over, and do the same to cook 3 more pancakes.

• Serve the pancakes on warmed plates, sprinkled with sugar. Decorate with a fresh mint sprigs.

●

Serving suggestions: Serve with a dollop of whipped cream or a scoop of ice cream.

Variations: Use raspberries or blackberries in place of blueberries. Use wholewheat flour in place of white flour.

Chocolate Noodles with Vanilla Sauce

An unusual and sumptuous dessert of hot, sweet noodles for you and your guests to enjoy.

Preparation time: 20 minutes, plus 30 minutes resting time · Cooking time: 15 minutes · Serves: 4

1½ cups	plain flour, sifted	375 mL
1 cup	cocoa powder, sifted	250 mL
⅓ cup	icing sugar, sifted	75 mL
2	large eggs	2
2 oz	Mascarpone cheese	50 g
	a large pinch of salt	
3 tbsp	butter	45 mL
3½ tbsp	granulated sugar	50 mL
4	egg yolks	4
6 tbsp	caster (superfine) sugar	90 mL
¾ cup + 2 tbsp	milk	200 mL
⅔ cup	heavy cream	150 mL
1	vanilla pod (or 3–4 drops of extract)	1
	fresh mint sprigs, to decorate	

• For the dough, place the flour, cocoa powder, icing sugar, eggs, cheese and salt together in a bowl and mix well. Knead gently for about 5–10 minutes, or until a smooth dough has formed.

• Cover and set aside to rest for 30 minutes.

• Bring a large saucepan of water to the boil and add the butter and granulated sugar.

• Roll out the dough on a lightly floured work surface and cut into thin strips.

• Add strips to the boiling water and simmer for about 4 minutes, until just tender, then drain, pat dry with absorbent kitchen paper or a clean tea-towel and keep warm.

• For the sauce: in a bowl, beat the egg yolks with the caster sugar and set aside.

• Place the milk and cream in a saucepan with the vanilla pod and stir for a few minutes. Remove the vanilla pod.

• Heat the milk and cream gently, stirring, then pour onto the egg mixture, stirring continuously.

• Return to the pan and heat gently, stirring continuously, until the sauce thickens. Do not allow the mixture to boil.

• Serve the warm chocolate noodles on dishes with the vanilla sauce poured over. Garnish with fresh mint sprigs.

Serving suggestion: Serve with fresh fruit such as raspberries, strawberries or cherries.

Variation: Use a few drops of vanilla extract added to the warmed milk and cream mixture, in place of the vanilla pod.

Steamed Almond Pudding

A deliciously light and moist steamed sponge pudding — ideal for a family dessert.

Preparation time: 15 minutes · Cooking time: 1–1½ hours · Serves: 4–6

7 tbsp	butter, softened	105 mL
1 cup	caster (superfine) sugar	250 mL
1 tbsp	light brown sugar	15 mL
3	medium eggs	3
	a pinch of salt	
2	drops of almond extract	2
½ cup	chopped almonds or hazelnuts	125 mL
1¼ cups	plain flour, sifted	300 mL
5 tbsp	cornstarch	75 mL
2 tsp	baking powder, sifted	10 mL
3 tbsp	milk	45 mL
	a little flour, for dusting	

• Beat the butter in a bowl until creamy, then gradually beat in the caster sugar, brown sugar, eggs, salt and almond extract.

• Stir in the nuts, then fold in the flour, cornstarch and baking powder. Stir in the milk and mix well.

• Grease a metal salad bowl and dust with a little flour.

• Spoon the almond mixture into the bowl and level the surface.

• Cover with greased wax paper and secure with string.

• Steam in a steamer over a pan of boiling water for 1–1½ hours, or until risen and cooked.

• Turn out onto a warmed serving plate and serve immediately.

●

Serving suggestions: Serve with chocolate sauce or zabaglione.

Variations: Use vanilla extract in place of almond extract. Use currants or sultana raisins in place of nuts. Use half white and half wholewheat flour in place of all white flour.

Chocolate and Almond Cookies

These tempting little crunchy cookies are a real treat. Perfect for serving after dinner with coffee.

Preparation time: 40 minutes, plus overnight chilling time · Cooking time: 12–15 minutes · Makes: about 50

3 cups	plain white flour	750 mL
2 tsp	baking powder	10 mL
¾ cup	caster (superfine) sugar	175 mL
1 tbsp	light brown sugar	15 mL
	a pinch of salt	
1	large egg, beaten	1
¾ lb	cold butter, diced	350 g
½ cup	cocoa powder, sifted	125 mL
1 tbsp	caster sugar	15 mL
1 tbsp	milk or rum	15 mL
⅓ cup	coarsely chopped blanched almonds	75 mL
	a little egg white, for brushing	

- Sift the flour and baking powder into a bowl and mix well.

- Make a well in the center and add ¾ cup (175 mL) sugar, brown sugar, salt and egg and mix well.

- Rub in the butter a little at a time and gradually knead the mixture to form a smooth dough.

- Set aside about one third of the dough.

- Add the cocoa powder, 1 tbsp (15 mL) caster sugar, milk or rum and the chopped almonds to the remaining dough, kneading well.

- Form the dough into 4 rectangular sausage shapes about 12½ in (31 cm) long, 1¼ in (3 cm) wide and about ⅝ in (1.5 cm) thick.

- Roll out the reserved dough to about 17½ in (44 cm) by 12½ in (31 cm) and cut into 4 strips, each about 4¼ in (11 cm) by 12½ in (31 cm).

- Brush the dough with a little egg white and place one sausage of almond-flavored dough on each piece of plain dough and wrap the plain dough around the flavored dough, enclosing it completely.

- Wrap each 'loaf' in aluminum foil and chill overnight in the refrigerator.

- Unwrap the loaves, cut into ½-in (1-cm) slices and place on greased baking trays covered with greaseproof or non-stick baking paper.

- Bake in a preheated oven at 400°F/200°C for 12–15 minutes, until cooked.

- Transfer to a wire rack to cool before serving.

Serving suggestions: Serve with a glass of dessert wine or freshly squeezed fruit juice.

Variations: Use half white and half wholewheat flour in place of all white flour. Use hazelnuts or pecan nuts in place of almonds.

COOK'S TIP

Store the cold, cooked cookies in an airtight container to keep them as fresh as possible.

Brown Bread Ice Cream

This homemade ice cream makes a delicious, refreshing dessert.

Preparation time: 15 minutes, plus freezing time · Cooking time: 20 minutes · Serves: 4

⅓ cup	brown breadcrumbs	75 mL
⅓ cup	brown sugar	75 mL
2	large eggs, separated	2
1¼ cups	thick-set plain yogurt	300 mL
2 tsp	honey (optional)	10 mL

• Place the breadcrumbs on a baking sheet and cover with the sugar.

• Bake in a preheated oven at 375°F/190°C for 20 minutes, or until beginning to brown and caramelize. Stir once or twice to brown evenly. Remove and set aside to cool.

• In a bowl, whisk the egg whites until stiff.

• In a separate bowl, stir the egg yolk into the yogurt, then fold in the egg white. Add the honey, if using, and fold in evenly.

• Fold in the cooled breadcrumbs and mix well. Spoon into a shallow, freezer-proof container.

• Cover and freeze for 1–2 hours, or until mushy in consistency.

• Turn into a chilled bowl and beat with a fork or whisk to break down the ice crystals. Return to the freezer container, cover and store in freezer.

• Transfer to the refrigerator for 30 minutes before serving, to soften a little. Serve in scoops.

Serving suggestion: Serve with wafer biscuits.

Variations: Use white breadcrumbs in place of brown breadcrumbs. Use strained cottage cheese or whipped heavy cream in place of plain yogurt. Use maple syrup in place of honey.

Mixed Seed Bread Rolls

These seed-topped bread rolls make a delicious snack at any time of the day. Serve freshly baked, warm or cold.

Preparation time: 20 minutes, plus kneading and rising time · Cooking time: 15–20 minutes · Makes: about 12

3 cups	white bread flour	750 mL
½ cup	lukewarm milk	125 mL
	a large pinch of sugar	
2	packets (¼ oz/8 g each) dry yeast	2
7 tbsp	butter, at room temperature	105 mL
2	medium eggs	2
1 tbsp	salt	15 mL
2–3 tbsp	olive oil	30–45 mL
2	egg yolks	2
1 tbsp	caraway seeds	15 mL
1 tbsp	coarse sea salt	15 mL
1 tbsp	coriander seeds	15 mL

COOK'S TIP

•

Use a mixer with a dough hook attachment to mix and knead the bread dough, to save a little time and effort.

• Sift the flour into a bowl. Add the milk, stir in the sugar, then sprinkle the yeast into the mixture.

• Mix to a smooth dough, knead gently, then leave to rise for 10–15 minutes.

• Add the butter, 2 whole eggs, salt and 1–2 tbsp (15–30 mL) of the oil to the dough and work into the dough until well mixed and smooth.

• Cover the dough and set aside in a warm place for about 30 minutes to rise.

• Knead the dough once more and set aside for a further 30 minutes.

• Divide the dough into about 12 small balls, then roll each out on a lightly floured work surface.

• Grease a baking sheet with the remaining oil. Place the dough balls on the baking sheet and flatten each one out slightly.

• In a bowl, beat the 2 egg yolks with ¼ cup (60 mL) water and brush the dough balls with the mixture.

• Sprinkle the dough balls with caraway seeds, salt and coriander seeds. Leave for a further 10 minutes to rise.

• Bake in a preheated oven at 350°F/180°C for 15–20 minutes, until risen, cooked and golden brown. Serve warm or cold.

•

Serving suggestions: Serve spread with butter, hummus spread (see page 106) or vegetarian paté.

Variations: Use wholewheat flour or a mixture of white and wholewheat flour in place of all white flour. Use cumin, poppy or sesame seeds in place of caraway seeds.

Autumn Loaf

This potato bread is ideal served freshly baked and still warm for a welcome snack.

Preparation time: 40 minutes, plus kneading and rising times · Cooking time: 40–50 minutes · Makes: 2 x 1-lb (450-g) loaves

3	medium-large russet or Idaho potatoes	3
2½	packets (¼ oz/8 g each) dry yeast	2½
3 cups	wholewheat bread flour	750 mL
¾ cup + 2 tbsp	lukewarm milk	200 mL
3 tbsp	butter, softened	45 mL
1 tsp	sea salt	5 mL
1	apple	1
1¼ cups	sunflower seeds	300 mL

• Wash the potatoes, then cook in a large saucepan of lightly salted, boiling water for about 20 minutes, until tender.

• Peel the potatoes while they are still hot, then mash well. Set aside.

• Dissolve the yeast in 2–3 tbsp (30–45 mL) lukewarm water in a bowl. Mix the yeast with the flour in a large bowl, then add the milk, a further ¾ cup (175 mL) lukewarm water and the butter. Add the salt, then knead well to form a smooth dough.

• Peel and core the apple, then finely grate.

• Heat all but 2 tbsp (30 mL) of the sunflower seeds in a pan without any oil or fat for 5 minutes, then knead into the dough, together with the mashed potatoes and grated apple.

• Place the dough in a bowl, cover and set aside in a warm place for about 1½ hours to rise.

• Grease two 1-lb (450-g) loaf tins, divide the dough equally between them, then sprinkle with the remaining 2 tbsp (30 mL) sunflower seeds and leave to rise in a warm place for a further 40 minutes.

• Bake in a preheated oven at 425°F/220°C for about 40–50 minutes, until cooked. When cooked, turn the bread out of the tins on its side and place on a wire rack to cool. Serve in slices.

Serving suggestions: Serve in slices, warm or cold, spread with a little butter, vegetable margarine or savory vegetable paté.

Variations: Use sweet potatoes in place of standard potatoes. Use pumpkin, sesame or poppy seeds in place of sunflower seeds. Use 1 pear in place of the apple.

Index